Greenhouses

Created and designed by
the editorial staff of
ORTHO BOOKS

Project Manager
Cynthia Putnam

Manuscript Editor
Susan Lang

Consulting Editors
Doc and Katy Abraham

Writers
T. Jeff Williams
Larry Hodgson

Photographers
Saxon Holt
Michael Landis

Illustrators
Ron Hildebrand
Pamela Manley

Photography Editor
Roberta Spieckerman

Designer
Gary Hespenheide

Ortho Books

Publisher
Edward A. Evans

Editorial Director
Christine Jordan

Production Director
Ernie S. Tasaki

Managing Editors
Robert J. Beckstrom
Michael D. Smith
Sally W. Smith

System Manager
Linda M. Bouchard

Product Manager
Richard E. Pile, Jr.

Distribution Specialist
Barbara F. Steadham

Operations Assistant
Georgiann Wright

Administrative Assistant
Francine Lorentz-Olson

Technical Consultant
J. A. Crozier, Jr., Ph.D.

Address all inquiries to:
Ortho Books
Box 5006
San Ramon, CA 94583-0906

Copyright © 1978, 1991
Monsanto Company
All rights reserved under international and
Pan-American copyright conventions.

8	9	10	11
97	98	99	

ISBN 0-89721-229-0
Library of Congress Catalog Card
Number 90-84633

THE SOLARIS GROUP
2527 Camino Ramon
San Ramon, CA 94583

Acknowledgments

Copy Chief
Melinda E. Levine

Editorial Coordinator
Cass Dempsey

Copyeditor
John Hammett

Proofreader
Deborah Bruner

Indexer
Trisha Feuerstein

Editorial Assistant
John Parr

Composition by
Nancy P. Wilson-McCune
Laurie A. Steele

Layout and Production by
Studio 165

Separations by
Color Tech Corp.

Lithographed in the USA by
Banta Company

Special Thanks to
Alberta Agriculture
Amdega Conservatories, Inc.
John W. Bartok
Rosalie and Stanton Bier
Virginia Blakelock, Hobby Greenhouse Association
Busy-Bee Pre-School
Professor Edward Carnegie
College of Agriculture, Univ. of Illinois
Creative Structures, Inc.
E. C. Geiger Corporation
Environmental Research Laboratory, Univ. of Arizona
Filon Corporation
Angela and Jeff Finder
Fiske Landscaping, Inc.
Gardener's Supply
Gothic Arch Greenhouses
Dr. Harold Gray, National Greenhouse
  Manufacturers Association
Robert M. Hamilton
Instructor Magazine
Janco Greenhouses, J. A. Nearing Company
Michael Kosket
John J. Leathers
David Loring
Mr. and Mrs. Patrick Lubin
Machin Designs (USA), Inc.
Al and Marjie Molakidis
Pat Morgan
Leta and Victor Nelson
Jim Nybakken
Pacific Aquaculture
Pacific Coast Greenhouse Manufacturing
Progressive Building Products
Sturdi-Built Greenhouse Manufacturing
Texas Greenhouse Company
Carl Totemeier, Old Westbury Gardens
Tuggey's Hardware
21st Century Gardener
Sharon and Michael Ward

Photographers
Names of photographers are followed by the page
numbers on which their work appears. R=right,
C=center, L=left, T=top, B=bottom.

Amdega Conservatories, Inc.: 29
William C. Aplin: 66
Bill Apton: 6, 68B
M. Baker: 82L
John Blaustein: 44–45, back cover BR
Josephine Coatsworth: 8B, 43
Creative Structures Inc.: 61
Lois Engle: 108L, 108R
Douglas C. Evans: 17L, back cover TR
Barbara Ferguson: 83TR
Gardener's Supply: 67B
GE Lexan ® Thermoclear™: 16B, back cover BL
Gothic Arch Greenhouses: 16TR
Saxon Holt Photography: Cover, title page, 4–5, 18–19,
  58–59, 70–71, 75L, 96–97
©Jerry Howard, 1990/Positive Images: 7, 14
Tony Howarth: 11B, 25B, 35, 64R, 65, 69B
Sandra Ivany: 51L, 72R
Janco Greenhouses, J. A. Nearing Company: 50, 52
Michael Landis: 13BL, 16TL, 24T, 24B, 32, 56B, 74B,
  78, 84–85, 86B, 98L, 103A, 103B, 105
Machin Designs (USA) Inc.: 31
Michael McKinley: 81, 83TL
James Napton: 37
Ortho Photo Library: 10, 11T, 11C, 17R, 20, 21L, 21R,
  22, 25T, 33 all, 49, 54, 56, 64L, 67T, 69T, 73L,
  75R, 77R, 79, 82R, 83B, 88L, 88R, 90, 92 all, 93,
  98R, 101, 107, back cover TL
Pacific Coast Greenhouse Manufacturing Company:
  51R, 86T
Pamela Peirce: 8T, 102 all
Sturdi-Built Greenhouse Manufacturing Company:
  13T, 26, 48, 60, 68T, 72, 77L
Texas Greenhouse Company: 15, 55, 74T
©Michael S. Thompson, 1989/Comstock, Stock
  Photography: 46
Tom Tracy: 47

Photo Locations Provided by:
Fiske Landscaping, Inc.: Cover, title page
Pacific Coast Greenhouse Manufacturing Company:
  4–5, 18–19, 51R, 86T, 96–97
Sturdi-Built Greenhouse Manufacturing Company:
  13T, 26, 48, 58–59, 60, 68T, 72, 77L

Front Cover
Shade cloth is draped over the roof rails on this
redwood-and-glass kit greenhouse during very sunny,
hot weather.

Title Page
Wire mesh is often used for bench tops in
greenhouses.

Back Cover
Top left: An attached greenhouse can be an
attractive extension of your home.

Top right: Despite snowy weather outside, plants
inside a greenhouse will flourish if given the right
temperature, humidity, and light.

Bottom left: Polycarbonate panels are among the
plastic products gaining popularity as greenhouse
glazing.

Bottom right: Plants requiring long days and short
nights can be forced into bloom with artificial lights.

Greenhouses

Getting Started

With scores of building plans and kits available today, choosing the right greenhouse requires careful thought and planning.

The world of greenhouses is a world of magic, a world in which seasons and climates don't matter. In a greenhouse, flowers bloom the year around, exotic fruits thrive, and fresh vegetables are ripe for picking in winter.

The lure of the greenhouse is powerful. When you walk inside, you shut yourself off from a frenzied world outside. You work in the soil and putter around even during cold or stormy weather. You can tend orchids amid snow flurries and pot up plants during torrential downpours. You get a chance to grow species you've never grown before and try new gardening techniques in a pleasant, controlled environment.

In the past, greenhouses were a luxury for the wealthy, but today anyone can become part of this magical world. So strong is the interest in greenhouse gardening that there are now more than two million hobby greenhouses in the United States, and the number is expected to exceed three million by the end of the decade.

There are scores of models to choose from; you can build your own, or you can buy a prefabricated model only requiring assembly. Careful planning will ensure that your new greenhouse is exactly suited to your needs. Before purchasing materials or a kit, you must select an appropriate location where the light is conducive to greenhouse gardening, and you must decide what type of greenhouse you want: the size, style, and covering.

This handsome wood, glass, and stucco greenhouse blends architecturally with the house to which it is attached. In addition, brick paving links the greenhouse with the patio.

A wide variety of exotic and native plants are raised in the greenhouses at Bailey Arboretum in Locust Valley, New York.

GREENHOUSES THROUGH HISTORY

Greenhouses have come a long way since the wealthy in Europe and America used them to force oranges and pineapples in glass structures known as orangeries and pineries. During the mid-nineteenth century, the conservatory developed into a status symbol as well as a practical way to produce almost any crop or plant indoors.

Modern hobby greenhouses more closely resemble the commercial hothouses, rather than the beautiful conservatories, of that era. But today's greenhouse enjoys a tradition dating back much earlier than the last century; its roots go back some two thousand years.

One of the earliest known greenhouses was built around 30 A.D. for the Roman emperor Ti-

berius. Glass had not been invented and the greenhouse, then called a specularium, was painstakingly fabricated from small translucent sheets of mica. All this was done just to satisfy the emperor's craving for cucumbers out of season.

Tiberius's greenhouse hardly created a new rage. Not only was the expense prohibitive, but the technology of the greenhouse was in its infancy. It took centuries to evolve.

It was not until 1599 that the first practical greenhouse was built. Designed by a French botanist, Jules Charles, and constructed in Leiden, Holland, it was intended as a place for growing tropical plants for medicinal purposes. One of the favorite plants of the day was the tamarind, or Indian date, whose fruit was made into a curative drink.

The greenhouse idea caught on and began spreading throughout Europe. The French, who had a passion for that wonderful new fruit, the orange, began setting up structures—naturally enough, called orangeries—to protect their trees from frost. These structures were cumbersome. One built by Solomon de Caus in Heidelberg around 1619 had removable roof shutters that had to be put up and taken down daily during the frost season. This was no small chore considering that 340 orange trees were under the roof.

Experiments to improve the greenhouse concept, including angled glass walls and heating flues, continued throughout the seventeenth century. New building technology and improved glass led to larger and larger greenhouses that housed plants just to please the eyes and palates of European royalty.

The palace of Versailles was an example of the elaborate efforts of the aristocracy to build bigger and more spectacular orangeries. The Versailles orangery was more than 500 feet long, 42 feet wide, and 45 feet high, with south-facing windows for light and heat.

In Russia, Czar Alexander I was not to be outdone. Between 1801 and 1805, he built three parallel greenhouses in St. Petersburg, each 700 feet long and connected on each end by two more greenhouses of the same length. Sections for tropical plants and fruits towered 40 feet high. The entire structure was heated during the bitter Russian winters by furnaces fueled by birch wood.

Using organic gardening techniques and no heating fuels, the owner of this greenhouse in Martha's Vineyard gets exceptionally high yields of vegetables and flowers throughout the year. The eggs are from chickens that provide heat, CO_2, and compost fertilizer.

Right: Tunnel-type commercial greenhouses flank the colorful flower fields of Goldsmith Seeds in Gilroy, California. Bottom: Greenhouse design reached its peak during the Victorian age. Ornate Victorian-style greenhouses can still be found in public gardens and arboretums throughout the world.

Despite the elaborateness of these structures, it was the Victorian age in England that ushered in the golden era of the greenhouse. By the mid-nineteenth century, glass was being manufactured in great quantity and the prohibitive taxes on it were repealed. The wealthy immediately began competing with each other to build the most elaborate greenhouse, again primarily just to house citrus fruits and rare flowers. Little thought was given to using the greenhouse for a complete range of food production.

The soaring conservatory at Kew Gardens in England is a prime example of the Victorian greenhouse. A replica, the Conservatory of Flowers, is located in San Francisco's Golden Gate Park.

In America the first greenhouse on record was built around 1737 by Andrew Faneuil, a wealthy Boston merchant. Like his European predecessors, Faneuil used it primarily to grow fruit. The concept spread slowly, since almost all greenhouses were built for the wealthy. Indeed, George Washington, perhaps the richest American of his day, craved pineapples and

This solarium provides year-round enjoyment for its owners. Although plants play a decorative role, the structure is designed primarily for the comfort of people.

ordered a greenhouse pinery built at Mount Vernon so that he could serve fresh pineapple to his guests.

By 1825, however, greenhouses were increasingly common. Many of the greenhouses were heated by furnace-warmed air; some were pit greenhouses built into the earth and heated largely by sunlight flowing in south-facing windows. This is a design that remains highly practical today (see page 93).

Indeed, the modern concept of the greenhouse is simple and practical. No longer is it the private domain of the monied class but something that anyone can have for relatively little cost.

Today a greenhouse can go virtually anywhere there is space; it can be attached to the house, placed in the backyard, or perched on a roof or deck. In addition, greenhouse routines are now increasingly automated, reducing the amount of time and care owners must spend. Home production of all kinds of vegetables and flowers has never been quite as easy—or as pleasurable.

Solariums

The solarium, or sunroom, has become a popular living space in modern homes. Unlike a working greenhouse, it is not specifically designed as a structure for growing plants. However, there is no reason that a solarium can't be used for gardening in addition to being a place to relax and entertain.

Plants are generally used to decorate solariums. Because of the bright light and sunshine, most plants grow better in a solarium than they do in other parts of the house. Still, the light, temperature, and humidity levels in a solarium are set for the comfort of people, and you must choose plants that will adapt to these levels.

The best location for a sunroom is a southern exposure. A solarium in an eastern exposure, which gets morning sun, makes a good breakfast room. If set in a western exposure, a solarium will probably need shading from the hot summer sun. Unlike a greenhouse, a solarium can be located in a northern exposure. Since most of the light will be indirect, you will have to stock it with plants that tolerate low light.

For maximum light and views, solariums are usually covered with glass, although a rigid plastic glazing is possible. Tinted glass is sometimes used in very sunny areas where glare is a problem.

Some homeowners convert an existing room into a solarium; others add the structure to the house. As with greenhouses, you can build your own solarium from a plan or erect one from a kit. With the growing popularity of solariums, many greenhouse manufacturers have added prefabricated models to their product lines.

Many gardeners get a jump on the season by starting plants in a cold frame. This bottomless box made from wood and glass provides a protected environment for salad greens early in spring.

Cold Frames and Hotbeds

Years ago when a greenhouse was considered a luxury of the rich, many people owned what was sometimes called a poor man's greenhouse: a cold frame or hotbed built from scrap lumber and glass. These devices are nothing more than miniature greenhouses.

Many hobby greenhouse owners like either device as an adjunct to their greenhouse. For those who turn off the heat in the greenhouse during the coldest months, a hotbed provides a small growing area that can be inexpensively heated. A cold frame is an excellent place to acclimate greenhouse-grown plants before transplanting them into the garden.

You can assemble either structure from a kit, or you can easily build your own. Both cold frames and hotbeds can be fitted with an electrical heat-sensitive mechanism that opens and closes the cover when the temperature reaches preset highs and lows. The mechanism is available from greenhouse equipment suppliers.

Cold Frames
A cold frame is basically a bottomless wooden box placed on the ground (or sunk into the ground a foot or so) and filled with a good quality soil mix. The size of the box is up to you, but the sides needn't be taller than 10 inches.

The essential part of a cold frame is a slanting roof consisting of some type of transparent or semitransparent cover. In the past the most common covers were sash windows and, more often than not, the size of the cold frame was dictated by whatever extra windows were available. Windows are still perfectly acceptable covers, but many gardeners prefer either rigid or film plastic products. The cover should be adjustable to admit varying amounts of fresh air.

In cold-winter areas, cold frames work best for the early starting of hardy and half-hardy annuals. The temperature inside a cold frame is usually insufficient to germinate and protect seedlings of tender annuals.

Hotbeds
A hotbed is a cold frame with a source of heat inside. The heat source can be an electric heating cable, incandescent light bulbs, or manure.

To use a heating cable, dig out about 6 inches of topsoil below the frame and lay the cable so that the strands do not touch; place 6 inches of sand over the cable. To use incandescent bulbs, suspend eight 25-watt bulbs overhead. Heating a 6- by 6-foot hotbed uses about 80 kilowatts. To heat the hotbed with fresh manure, dig out an area below the frame about 10 to 12 inches deep. Fill this with the manure, then add 3 to 4 inches of soil on top.

Any of the heating methods above should keep plants from freezing unless the temperature dips below 10° F. In that case, cover the hotbed with a blanket.

PLANNING THE GREENHOUSE

Your greenhouse is more likely to be a practical structure suited to your needs if you think through the project first, before ordering any materials or starting work.

Since there are a host of possibilities open to you, it is important to make some decisions about the kind of greenhouse you want: the location, size, style, and covering. Then you must decide whether you want to build the greenhouse from a plan or buy a kit.

Assessing Your Needs

Your options will begin to narrow when you answer the following questions.

• How big a greenhouse do I need? Hobby greenhouse owners recommend making it larger than you anticipate using, because once you start greenhouse gardening you will probably want to expand. In many cases, available space will restrict the size of the greenhouse.

• What is my purpose in having a greenhouse? If your goal is to raise vegetables and flowers the year around, your needs will be different than if you want a greenhouse primarily for growing foliage houseplants. A warm greenhouse that permits maximum light and head room may be desirable for growing vegetables and flowers, but it isn't necessary for foliage houseplants.

• How elaborate a setup do I need, or want? If you require only an enclosed space where you can start plants from seed or grow a few species too tender for winters in your area, you may be satisfied with a small, simple, plastic greenhouse. If you view the greenhouse as an architectural feature, you may want a more elegant structure.

• Is a building permit necessary? Are there local design ordinances? Must the structure be set back a certain distance from property lines? Whether you are assembling a prefabricated greenhouse from a kit or constructing your own from a plan, you will probably need a building permit. Also, you will most likely need to adhere to certain construction specifications as well as to design and setback ordinances. Consult your local building department.

• Does a greenhouse mean higher property taxes? That depends on how taxes are levied locally. It may also depend on whether your greenhouse is classified as a permanent or temporary structure. Another consideration: In most areas greenhouses are no longer eligible for tax rebates on solar heating devices.

• How much does it cost to maintain a greenhouse and supply it with heat, water, and electric light? Depending on where you live, the heating cost can be very high, and it may dictate the size, shape, and construction of your greenhouse. Your local utility company can help estimate the cost of heating different types of greenhouse structures, or you may want to consider solar heating (see page 86).

A greenhouse can be located wherever there is enough space and sunlight. It can go underneath a stairway (top), on a rooftop (center), or in the backyard (bottom).

Locating the Greenhouse

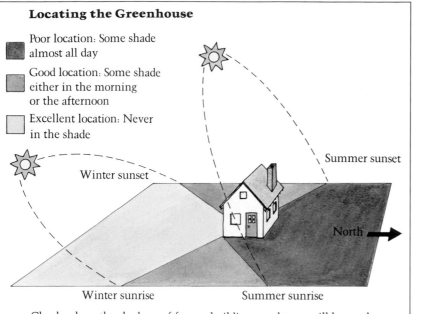

■ Poor location: Some shade almost all day

■ Good location: Some shade either in the morning or the afternoon

□ Excellent location: Never in the shade

Summer sunset

Winter sunset

North

Winter sunrise   Summer sunrise

Check where the shadows of fences, buildings, and trees will be cast by both the summer and winter sun. Locate the greenhouse where there is a minimum of shade

Selecting the Site

Deciding where to locate the greenhouse is a critical planning step. Unless it's a portable model built from a kit, the greenhouse is there to stay unless you are prepared to go to a lot of expense and effort to move it.

The first consideration is sunlight. It is important to locate the greenhouse where it will get the maximum amount of light possible. If it doesn't get at least six hours of direct sunlight a day, you will probably need to supplement the natural light with artificial light. The preferred exposure is southern; the next best exposures, in order of suitability for a greenhouse, are southeastern, southwestern, eastern, and western. A northern exposure is too shady for a greenhouse.

How the greenhouse is oriented is also important. An east-west greenhouse will transmit about 25 percent more light than one situated north-south, since it presents more surface to the sun at a right angle.

Take note of any trees, walls, fences, or other obstructions that may shut off light for a major portion of daylight hours. When considering this, remember that the sun will be much lower in the winter than in the summer. As a general rule, the distance of the greenhouse from a wall or other structure that might block sunlight should be equal to 2½ times the height of that structure.

A tree that will cast shade on the greenhouse isn't necessarily an obstacle. If the tree is deciduous—that is, drops its leaves in winter—it can provide shade during hot summer days but allow sunlight through when it's most needed in winter.

Drainage is another key consideration in selecting a site for the greenhouse. Don't locate it in a depression that will be a catch basin for rain and snow during the winter. Also avoid a boggy area where the soil is constantly wet.

Select a site that is relatively level or can easily be made level. If there is an incline behind the greenhouse, you may have to install tile or gravel ditches to divert runoff. If the site is well drained, you may choose to build a sun pit—a type of greenhouse with one wall built into the earth. See page 93 for details.

Access to water and electricity is another important factor in locating the greenhouse. The farther the structure is from these connections, the more laborious it is to run the utility lines there.

Consider, too, the difficulty in walking to your greenhouse during inclement weather. A structure near the house—or even better, attached to the house—is easy to tend during cold or rainy weather.

Choosing a Style

The style of greenhouse you select depends on such factors as how permanent you want the structure to be, whether it will be freestanding or attached to the house, your building skills, and the type of snow loads in your area.

You must also take into account the types of plants you will grow. For example, orchids can be grown in any type of structure, but tall shrubs and vines require a greenhouse with high supports. Therefore, an A-frame is not as usable as one of the other greenhouse styles.

The following are the major styles of greenhouses that can be built. Additional styles available in kits include the geodesic dome, the curved-roof, and the circular greenhouse.

Attached   Also called a lean-to, this type of greenhouse is an extension of the home. There is usually direct access from the house, and water and electricity are easily extended to the structure. In northern climates, an attached greenhouse should not be located under a sloping roof because of icicles or snow slides.

Left: This gambrel roof greenhouse comes unassembled in a kit. At least two people are needed to put it together; the time required depends on your manual skills. Bottom left: You can save money by building the greenhouse yourself from recycled materials. This attached wood and glass greenhouse is made from old window sashes. Bottom right: This gothic arch greenhouse is among the many styles available in kits. The aluminum framing and rigid plastic panels are provided by the manufacturer; the foundation should be prepared before the kit arrives.

This commercial greenhouse, also shown on page 7, enables the owner to produce organically grown vegetables the year around without any heating fuels. The A-frame design is particularly suited for shedding snow and capturing winter sunlight. A special ridge vent provides summer ventilation without any fans.

A-frame Simple to construct, the A-frame can be built in sections on the ground and then raised into place and covered. Although the shape is ideal for areas with heavy snow loads, it provides limited head room. Proper ventilation is also difficult to achieve.

Gothic arch The gothic roof line is made from laminated wood strips over which a permanent covering is installed. Extremely decorative, it is a challenging project, because the layout and lamination of the arches takes time. This style of greenhouse is a good choice for regions with heavy snow or rain; the curved sides keep precipitation from collecting.

Span roof This freestanding style probably has the most typical and usable shape of any greenhouse. The interior layout is extremely practical, and there is easy access for a loaded wheelbarrow through a door at either end. Both the snow-country model (see page 42) and the gambrel-roof models (see pages 39 and 41) are variations of the span-roof greenhouse.

Selecting the Covering

One of the most important decisions you must make is the choice of material to cover your greenhouse. You will want a material that lets in the maximum amount of light while allowing the least amount of heat to escape.

Greenhouse glazings have improved remarkably in recent years, and today the selection is the best it has ever been. In addition to glass, there is a wide range of plastic glazings in the form of film sheeting and rigid panels.

You may be confused by the many trade names for each type of plastic. Discuss your options with a reputable greenhouse supplier or builder, and make sure that the plastic is intended for greenhouse use.

Glass The traditional covering for greenhouses, glass is the preferred material for permanence. It lasts indefinitely, although it does become brittle with age. Since glass is breakable, it is more dangerous and difficult to install. It also requires a much sturdier frame than does a plastic-covered greenhouse.

Glass has undergone many improvements in recent years. Among the most important is increased strength (double- and triple-strength ratings) to resist breaking.

Larger panes are also available; because fewer structural members are needed, more light can enter the greenhouse. Also available are frosted and hammered panels to break up the light rays for more even distribution. Low-iron glass increases light, but its high cost is a deterrent.

Other advances have cut down on heat loss. Double-wall tempered glass reduces it by about one third. Low-emissivity, or low-e, coating, is another option; it reduces heat loss without a corresponding loss of light. In addition to being energy efficient, low-e glass reduces condensation, partially blocks ultraviolet rays, and makes the inside glass warmer to the touch.

Film plastic   A greenhouse covered with film plastic is one sixth to one tenth of the cost per square foot of a glass-covered structure. Although less permanent than glass, film plastic can be heated as efficiently as glass.

Previously, film plastic had a life span of approximately three months in summer and nine months in winter. Newer, clear types that resist yellowing last three to five years and allow up to 89 percent light transmission. Sold under many trade names, they are available in many thicknesses from 2 mil (.002 inch) to 15 mil (.015 inch). The thicker the film, the more expensive it is. Weather-resistant polyethylene film plastic, 4 mil thick (.004 inch), is perhaps the least expensive film plastic that makes a satisfactory covering for a hobby greenhouse.

In choosing among the many brand names of plastic sheeting, be sure to select one that is

A glass greenhouse requires a solid foundation. This prefabricated curved-roof structure sits securely on a concrete base.

Top left: This attached greenhouse uses three different glazings. Polyethylene plastic film cloaks glass louvers. In addition, fiberglass panels are used on the side of the structure.
Top right: The covering on this attached greenhouse is a combination of fiberglass and acrylic.
Bottom: Polycarbonate rigid panels cover this small freestanding greenhouse.

resistant to ultraviolet rays. You can also buy a film plastic with an infrared inhibitor; it cuts heat loss inside the greenhouse by up to 20 percent on a cloudless night. Another way to reduce heat loss is to double-layer the plastic, creating an air pocket for insulation. This space can be from ¾ to 4 inches thick. Although there is some reduction in light transmission, the heating cost is reduced by about one third.

Another innovation in film covering is an anticondensate additive that allows moisture buildup to run down the sides of the film instead of onto the plants. By removing the condensation drops that block the sun's rays, this new type of film plastic allows more light into the greenhouse. In addition, it helps stop disease infestation by keeping contaminated moisture from dripping on the plants.

Rigid plastics   These coverings, which include fiberglass, acrylic, and polycarbonate, come in corrugated and flat forms. Shatterproof, they resist hailstone damage. Some types of rigid plastics tend to get dirty and do not let in as much light as glass. However, all can be washed with detergent and water to remove the soil film.

All rigid plastics retain heat well. For example, fiberglass retains heat 4.4 times more efficiently than glass and 70.8 times more efficiently than polyethylene film. Plastic panels have fewer joint laps through which heat can escape. Corrugation in some types makes a very tight fit at lap joints, thus saving heat.

The total amount of light transmitted through fiberglass rigid panels is roughly equal to that transmitted through glass. Fiberglass actually has an advantage over glass because it transmits less heat. During the summer, a fiberglass greenhouse requires less cooling than a glass greenhouse of the same size.

Fiberglass coated with PVC (polyvinyl chloride) is a durable, relatively lightweight material that resists damage from weather, ultraviolet radiation, and acid rain.

Recent improvements in plastics include the introduction of structured sheets. Available in both acrylic and polycarbonate, these are double-skinned plastics separated by fins or veins for insulation. Although acrylic transmits light better, polycarbonate is stronger and more resistant to impact and fire. Both materials can be used on curved areas. Pure polycarbonate will quickly yellow in the sun, whereas acrylic retains its clarity longer. However, you can purchase ultraviolet-resistant polycarbonate.

Deciding Whether to Build or Buy

Once you know what kind of greenhouse you want, you must decide whether to build your own from a plan or assemble a prefabricated model from a kit.

Base your decision on such factors as your available time, budget, and building skills. If you want to construct your own but are too inexperienced, consider hiring a skilled carpenter to help you.

If saving money is your goal, you may be able to do that by building your own, especially if you are able to use scrap materials such as old windows and discarded doors. Even if you buy new materials, you can generally build for less than you can buy a comparable prefabricated structure.

On the other hand, if you have more money than you have construction skills, a kit may be the logical choice. You won't need the range of tools required for building from a plan, either. You can even add on to some kits once you've gained experience greenhouse gardening.

Kits provide everything you need—including a lightweight foundation for some models. Other kits are designed to sit on a solid foundation, and they require a great deal of preparatory work. You will have to construct the same foundation that you would need if you were building your own greenhouse from a plan.

Before deciding on a kit, send away for catalogs and study them carefully. You can ask the manufacturer for a set of assembly instructions before purchasing a kit. It is also a good idea to request the name of a nearby greenhouse owner who has the model you're interested in. Your decision may be easier when you see the greenhouse in operation. For more information about kits, see the third chapter.

Rather than build a greenhouse from a plan or assemble a prefabricated model from a kit, you may opt for a custom-built structure. Both the octagonal conservatory (left) and the shaded greenhouse (right) are the work of professional builders.

Building the Greenhouse

Here are building plans for several models— including an attached greenhouse and several freestanding types—that require varying degrees of carpentry skills.

Building your own greenhouse from scratch can be a challenging, rewarding experience. Not only do you have a feeling of accomplishment, but you can make changes as you go along—a common trait among builders.

There are dozens of styles—including attached, A-frame, gothic arch, and gambrel roof—to choose from. Pick a model that serves your gardening needs but also one that will not exhaust your time, budget, and building skills. If a plan does not meet your requirements exactly, feel free to use your own ingenuity—and perhaps advice from an experienced builder—to adapt it to your space and circumstances.

When selecting a suitable style, be sure to consider the two solar greenhouse models and the sun pit featured in the sixth chapter. You may prefer one of those designs.

Depending on the model you build, you may need a sturdy concrete foundation, or a lightweight substructure may be adequate. Instructions for both kinds are included.

The turning of the last screw marks the completion of this brand new wood-frame greenhouse built from a plan.

The type of foundation depends not only on the climate but also on the weight of the structure and the construction materials used. This greenhouse required a deep, solid foundation to support its heavy wood frame and extensive glass paneling.

CONSTRUCTING THE FOUNDATION

A foundation must be level and square if the greenhouse walls and roof are to fit properly. The following are step-by-step directions for establishing the boundaries of the greenhouse and building the footing, concrete-block foundation walls, and sill.

Laying Out the Site

After selecting the style and dimensions of your greenhouse, it is time to get to work. The first, and perhaps the most important, task is the site layout—a process to determine precisely where the outside edges of the foundation will be located. This is a critical step, because the walls and roofs won't fit properly unless the foundation is square.

The type of foundation required depends on the greenhouse and your climate. If you live in an area where the ground freezes during the winter and you intend to cover the greenhouse with glass, you will need to build a foundation that reaches below the frost line. In some areas this will be only 8 inches deep, and in other areas it may extend 4 or 5 feet below ground. If the footing is too shallow, the ground below may freeze and heave, cracking both the footing and the greenhouse.

A lightly framed, plastic-covered greenhouse in a mild climate can get by with a light foundation. See suggestions for lightweight foundations on page 22.

Select a level, or nearly level, site for the greenhouse. The footing, which extends below the frost line and is usually made from concrete, goes in first. The foundation wall goes on top of the footing, and the frame for the greenhouse sits on top of the wall. The general rule is that the footing should be twice the width of the foundation wall. Thus, if you plan to use standard 8-inch concrete blocks for the foundation wall, make the footing 16 inches wide.

Begin by driving a 2 by 2 stake into the ground at one corner of the greenhouse site. For a foundation wall 2 feet high, leave 2 feet of the stake above ground. This is point A. Measure off another corner and drive a stake there. This is point B. Drive a small nail in the top center of each stake and connect the nails with a tightly drawn string. This line represents one side of the greenhouse.

Measure the distance to a corner of the opposite wall, using a framing square to make it as close as possible to a 90-degree angle. Drive a temporary stake in at point C and connect B and C with string.

Now make sure that the AB and BC strings form an exact 90-degree angle. From point B toward point A, measure exactly 3 feet and mark it on the string with a felt pen. Now, from point B toward point C, measure off exactly 4 feet and mark it. For corner B to be square, there must be exactly 5 feet between the marks on the two strings. With a friend or two helping, adjust the stake at point C until the diagonal is exactly 5 feet.

For the fourth corner, measure as closely as you can and drive a temporary stake at corner D. Make sure the distance from A to D is the same as from B to C. Using the same trick of marking the strings at 3 feet and 4 feet, adjust the stake at point D until the diagonal measures exactly 5 feet.

Now, for the final proof that everything is square: Both diagonals, from A to C and from B to D, should be the same. Allowing for slack in the measuring tape and difficulty in measuring the string, a difference of ⅛ inch for a small structure or ¼ inch for a large one is allowable. If the difference in the diagonals is greater, then you need to adjust the layout.

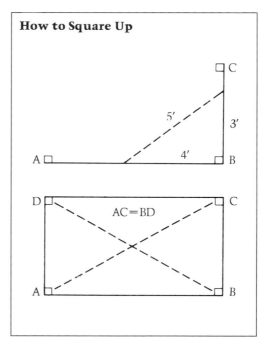

How to Square Up

Bottom, left and right: This greenhouse gardener is constructing the framework for a simple tunnel-type greenhouse that sits directly on the ground. The benderboard frame is attached to a foundation consisting of two 2 by 4s on top of each other. Polyethylene plastic film will be stretched over the framework.

Precast Pier Foundation

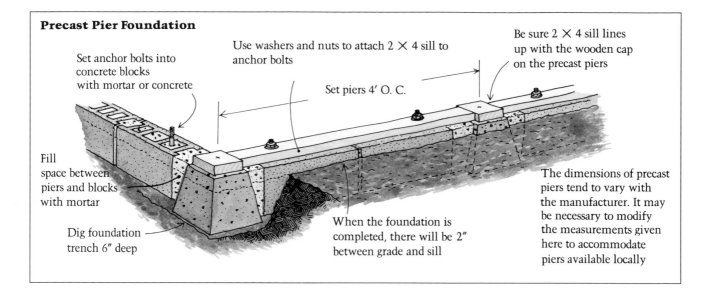

Set anchor bolts into concrete blocks with mortar or concrete

Use washers and nuts to attach 2 × 4 sill to anchor bolts

Be sure 2 × 4 sill lines up with the wooden cap on the precast piers

Set piers 4' O. C.

Fill space between piers and blocks with mortar

Dig foundation trench 6" deep

When the foundation is completed, there will be 2" between grade and sill

The dimensions of precast piers tend to vary with the manufacturer. It may be necessary to modify the measurements given here to accommodate piers available locally

Lightweight Foundations

A simple, lightly framed greenhouse with a plastic covering does not require an imposing foundation. An equally simple, lightweight foundation is adequate.

You can make a simple foundation from railroad ties. Either sink the ties to just above ground level, or place them on the ground and stake them with iron reinforcing rods (also called rerod bars, or rebars). The greenhouse is then anchored directly to this foundation.

Another easy foundation suitable for mild-winter areas starts with a 6-inch-deep ditch dug to the size of the greenhouse, then lined with concrete building blocks that you fill with concrete. Insert anchor bolts for the frame. An alternative is to sink precast concrete piers every 4 feet around the perimeter and build up from there.

A lightweight greenhouse like this one can sit directly on the ground in an arid, mild-winter climate.

Batter boards The stakes and string you just put up mark the exact outside measurements of the greenhouse. The next step is to lay out the footing. For this, batter boards are needed at the four corners. The batter boards will allow you to remove the stakes and strings when you dig the footing trench and still know exactly where the corners are.

Start by driving a 2 by 4 stake about 2 feet back from the corner stakes and directly on the diagonal from the opposite corner. Drive two more stakes 4 feet from the corner down each side of the building outline to form a 90-degree angle. Check the angle with a large framing square. Connect the stakes with 1 by 4 boards nailed flush with the top of the stakes. Use a level to check the boards.

Construct batter boards at the three remaining corners. These batter boards must all be at the same level. If you don't have a small hand transit to check, stretch the string tightly and check with a line level.

Now pull another set of strings directly on top of the original four strings and make small saw kerfs, or cuts, in the batter board to indicate the lines. Remove the original stakes and

Laying Out the Footing

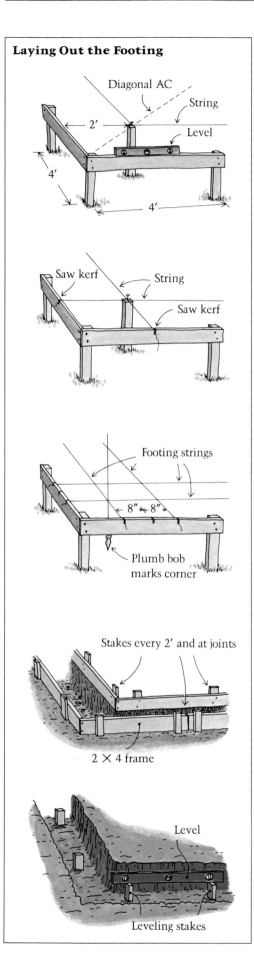

Diagonal AC

String

Level

2'

4'

4'

Saw kerf   String

Saw kerf

Footing strings

8" 8"

Plumb bob marks corner

Stakes every 2' and at joints

2 × 4 frame

Level

Leveling stakes

all of the strings. To locate the corners during the building process, simply stretch string tightly through the cuts on the batter boards; the intersections of the strings mark the corners of the greenhouse.

The footing You're ready to mark the outline for the footing. If you intend to build a concrete-block foundation wall, the footing should be 16 inches wide, or twice the width of the standard 8-inch concrete block. If you intend to erect the greenhouse directly on the footing, 12 inches wide will be ample. Check with your building department to find out about any local regulations.

For a 16-inch footing, mark off 8 inches on each side of the saw cuts in the batter boards; make additional saw cuts at these marks and pull strings all around. Using a plumb bob, drive small stakes at the inside and outside points for each corner. Now snap chalk lines on the ground to mark the footing; then remove the strings.

For an 8-inch footing that will support a foundation wall, make the trench 10 inches deep. This will keep the footing 2 inches below ground and out of sight.

However, if you plan to build directly on the footing, then bring it up above ground a few inches to keep the greenhouse walls clear of the ground. Do this by nailing together a 2 by 4 frame flush with the edges of the footing trench, inside and outside. Stake it every 2 feet for added strength since concrete is heavy and can easily bow out weak frames. The frame must be level all the way around before you pour the concrete.

For a footing that will remain 2 inches below the ground level, the big question is how to make it level when you pour the concrete. The answer is leveling stakes. For a footing 8 inches deep, start in the center of the trench at one corner and drive a 2 by 2 stake into the ground with exactly 8 inches showing. Now proceed around the trench, driving stakes every 4 to 7 feet with just 8 inches showing. Use a straight 2 by 4 stud and a carpenter's level to check each one. When you return to the original stake, you must still be on the same level. Now, when you pour exactly to the top of the stakes, you know your footing will be level. Don't worry about removing these stakes: Leave them in the concrete.

Pouring the Concrete

Line the bottom of the trench with large rocks. Not only do the rocks help bind the concrete, but the space they take up means there will be less concrete to pour. Some building codes may require laying concrete reinforcing rods, but this is not customary. Check with your local building department.

You can order ready-mixed concrete delivered to the site, or you can mix the concrete yourself in a wheelbarrow or a small mixer available at many equipment rental shops. Combine 1 shovel of portland cement, 2 shovels of sand, and 4 shovels of gravel. Mix thoroughly while dry, then slowly add water. Keep mixing and make sure that the entire mix gets wet. From this point it takes only a little more water until the mix is completely wet and loose without being runny.

After you have filled the footing trench to what appears to be the proper level, take a troweling tool and work the mix vigorously until all the air bubbles are out and the mix has settled. You may have to add more concrete. Work it again until all the gravel is below the surface and you have a smooth, level surface for the foundation blocks. For final smoothing, use a concrete float.

If you're going to attach the frame directly to the footing, insert the anchor bolts now. Leave 2½ inches of the threaded end exposed.

Top: A homemade plumb bob is used to determine the exact corners of the concrete-block foundation wall. Bottom: While the mortar is still damp, the joints are raked to remove excess mortar and to form a concave impression. Instead of purchasing a jointer, you can use a short length of ½-inch copper pipe.

Use a framing square to make sure the bolts are perpendicular.

If rain is expected, cover the footing with plastic sheeting. If there is danger of a freeze, cover with plastic or straw, or both. It will take at least three days for the footing to set enough so that the foundation walls can be started. Lightly sprinkle the concrete with water on the second and third days to prevent excessively rapid drying, which causes cracking.

The Foundation Walls

The foundation walls, or knee walls, of a greenhouse can be both attractive and functional. Usually 24 to 30 inches high, the walls keep rain and snow from wetting the sill.

Before starting the walls, you must find the exact outline and corners again. Put the strings back in the saw cuts in the batter boards and pull all the way around. To mark the corners, hang a plumb bob from the point where the strings intersect. Next, snap chalk lines from corner to corner on the footing.

The walls are usually made from concrete blocks 16 inches long, 8 inches high, and 8 inches wide. (Actually, all measurements are just ⅜ inch less so that you can lay ⅜ inch of mortar to bond the blocks.)

Start at one corner and lay the first block precisely. The wall will be determined by how square and level that first block is.

Use a mortar mix that is 1 part mortar (not portland) cement and 4 parts fine sand. Mix it dry and then add water until it is smooth and plastic, not runny. Trowel the mortar across the dampened footing and place the first block. Check to make sure it is level and square. Note that corner blocks have one flat end for facing, and the other blocks have two grooved ends for joining. You get a mixture of the two when you order blocks.

Lay the blocks for the four corners first, extending the bottom layer enough each time to support the next layer at the corners.

To join the blocks, stand one on end and butter, or coat, the exposed end with mortar, then fit it to the adjoining block. To join stacking blocks, butter the top of a block on the inside and outside edges, then lay the next block on top. It is not customary to butter the cross groove, but note that one end of it is wide and the other is narrow. The wide end always goes up so you can apply mortar to it.

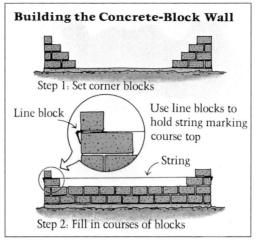

Building the Concrete-Block Wall

Step 1: Set corner blocks

Line block

Use line blocks to hold string marking course top

String

Step 2: Fill in courses of blocks

After the corners are up to the desired height, start laying the rest of the courses. To keep these level, use line blocks that hook over the ends of the blocks with a string stretched tightly between. You can also put perpendicular poles at each corner with marks every 8 inches for the strings.

Be sure to ask for some half-sized blocks when you place your initial order. These shortened blocks are needed at corners and they sometimes fit in the middle of the course. The

Top right: This simple foundation consists of redwood posts sunk in concrete; metal connectors join the studs to the posts. Concrete piers serve the same purpose but last longer.
Bottom: This glass greenhouse sits on a sturdy brick foundation.

more common case is that you have to cut a block to fit. Allow ½ inch on each end for the mortar and then cut the block by first scoring all around with a cold chisel and then snapping the block apart with the chisel and a hammer. Wear safety goggles for this.

Special blocks recessed to accept door jams are also available. You will need these for framing the door openings.

In cold-winter areas, you can insulate the wall by pouring silicone-treated vermiculite into the block cells as the blocks are being laid. (Never use untreated vermiculite.) For added insulation, polystyrene sheets can be fastened to the inside walls when completed. The 2 by 8 sheets, with reflective foil (usually aluminum) on one or both sides, are available in 1- and 2-inch thicknesses.

The Sill

The sill is a board—preferably 2 by 6 redwood or other rot-resistant lumber—that sits horizontally on top of the footing or foundation wall and provides a nailing surface for the greenhouse walls. The sill is bolted to the foundation with anchor bolts. Space the bolts 4 to 6 feet apart, always putting one near the end of each length of sill. Avoid putting a bolt where a stud will stand.

If you have a concrete-block wall, hold the concrete in place by pushing wads of paper down each opening where the anchor bolts will go. Fill the openings with concrete and anchor the bolts vertically in place. Leave 2½ inches of each bolt exposed.

When the concrete has set, place lengths of 2 by 6 lumber exactly in line over the foundation and then tap the sill with a hammer above each anchor bolt. Drill holes through each bolt mark. Once the sill is bolted in place, you're ready to start framing the greenhouse.

Anchoring the Sill

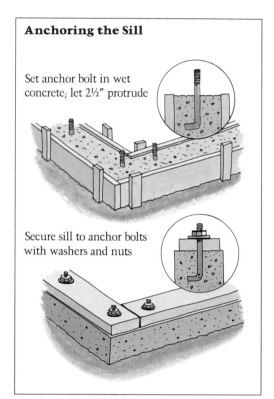

Set anchor bolt in wet concrete; let 2½" protrude

Secure sill to anchor bolts with washers and nuts

This wood and glass greenhouse rests on a tall concrete foundation wall.

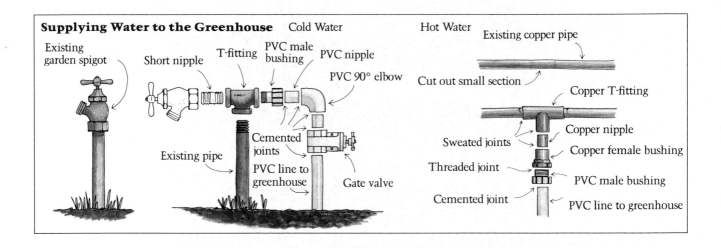

Supplying Water to the Greenhouse Cold Water   Hot Water

Existing garden spigot | Short nipple | T-fitting | PVC male bushing | PVC nipple | PVC 90° elbow | Cemented joints | Existing pipe | PVC line to greenhouse | Gate valve

Existing copper pipe | Cut out small section | Copper T-fitting | Copper nipple | Copper female bushing | Sweated joints | Threaded joint | PVC male bushing | Cemented joint | PVC line to greenhouse

Water and Electrical Hookups

Plan your water and electrical connections before you pour concrete for the footing. In most cases, waiting until the foundation is built makes the task more difficult.

Installing Water Lines
It is preferable to run the water lines to the greenhouse entirely underground. This way they won't freeze in the winter and there will be no unsightly pipes showing. If you live in an area where the ground freezes, check with a local plumber or hardware store for the proper depth to lay the pipes.

Before pouring concrete for the footing, lay the pipes in a trench that runs under the footing. You don't have to fully install the water lines: Just lay in a section of PVC (polyvinyl chloride) pipe that you can connect later. If you forget or already have a greenhouse foundation, you can dig down and then shove the PVC pipe through, since it is quite flexible.

If you want to run a water pipe through a concrete-block wall, first, on the block, score a circle slightly larger than the pipe. Tap it out with a cold chisel and run the pipe through. Use a mortar mix to fill the hole around the pipe.

The only complication in hooking up water lines comes in tying into the main supply line. Whether you do this outside or have to go under the house, the easiest water pipe material to work with is PVC. The pipe comes in a variety of sizes and strengths; schedule 40 pipe is more than adequate to withstand residential water pressures. The plastic cuts easily

and glues together in seconds. It is also flexible and can go around curves or under footings.

Cold water   If you are in an area with little or no freezing and you want only a cold water tap in the greenhouse, the easiest way to get water is to hook into an outside spigot. Check the size of the spigot pipe and note whether it has male or female fittings. Buy the proper T-fitting for the spigot. With the water supply shut off, attach the fitting and screw the spigot back on one side.

Your greenhouse line will come from the other side. The line can be as small as ½ inch if water must move only a short distance. A ¾-inch line will give you more water. If the water must travel 100 feet or more, use 1-inch PVC pipe.

To hook up the greenhouse water line, screw a PVC bushing onto the T-fitting. Glue a short length of PVC pipe into that and add a 90-degree elbow that points straight down. From this elbow run pipe into the ground and over to the greenhouse.

Install a shut-off valve above the ground inside the greenhouse. This will allow you to turn off the water to the greenhouse without affecting your water supply elsewhere.

Hot water   In cold regions where tap water is only a few degrees above freezing in winter, you may want to supply hot water to the greenhouse. You can do this by tying into the hot water–heater supply lines in your house or by installing a tankless water heater in the greenhouse.

In many cases, the house hot-water lines are copper pipes. To connect PVC to

copper you must install a copper T-fitting in the pipes. Doing this requires moderate skill in using a propane torch and solder to sweat the fittings.

A tankless, or instant, water heater gives you access to both cold and hot water. It is efficient because it produces hot water only when you need it. When you open the hot water faucet, heating elements are activated instantly. When you turn off the faucet, the heat shuts off.

Making Electric Connections
Unless you are experienced in working with electricity, this phase of construction requires an expert. An electrician's knowledge is needed in determining how much power is required in your greenhouse and whether a hookup can be made on your existing panel or whether a separate meter and panel are needed. When lights, fans, and heating cables under propagation beds all operate at once, they draw considerable power.

If you decide to hire an electrician, you can save money by doing the preliminary work yourself. Check with the local building department for the size of the electrical wire needed and then buy the necessary supplies. Any electric outlets for either inside or outside the greenhouse should be weatherproof to prevent shock. The electrical circuits should be protected by ground fault circuit interrupters.

Dig a trench at least 3 feet deep from the greenhouse to the power source; lay the wire in plastic conduit tubing in the trench. With those steps completed, the electrician can complete the hookup quickly.

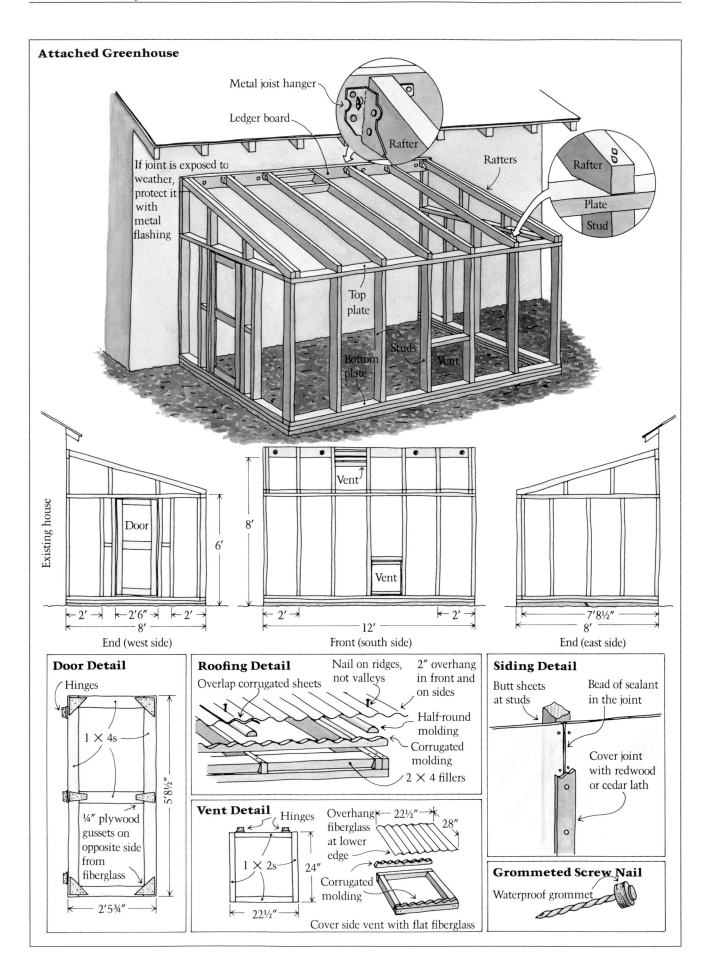

Attached Greenhouse

Metal joist hanger

Ledger board

Rafter

Ratters

If joint is exposed to weather, protect it with metal flashing

Rafter

Plate

Stud

Top plate

Bottom plate

Studs

Vent

Existing house

Door

6'

2' — 2'6" — 2'

8'

End (west side)

Vent

8'

Vent

2' — 12' — 2'

Front (south side)

7'8½"

8'

End (east side)

Door Detail

Hinges

1 × 4s

5'8½"

¼" plywood gussets on opposite side from fiberglass

2'5¾"

Roofing Detail

Overlap corrugated sheets

Nail on ridges, not valleys

2" overhang in front and on sides

Half-round molding

Corrugated molding

2 × 4 fillers

Vent Detail

Hinges

1 × 2s

24"

22½"

Overhang fiberglass at lower edge

22½"

28"

Corrugated molding

Cover side vent with flat fiberglass

Siding Detail

Butt sheets at studs

Bead of sealant in the joint

Cover joint with redwood or cedar lath

Grommeted Screw Nail

Waterproof grommet

ATTACHED GREENHOUSE

The most practical of all greenhouses is one that becomes a part of your own house. Construction is easier—and the structure is better braced—because one wall of the greenhouse is actually your house wall.

This 8- by 12-foot lean-to is framed with 2 by 4 redwood and covered with rigid plastic panels. Once the foundation is constructed and all the supplies are on hand, two people can complete the greenhouse in a weekend. The construction can be built around a door or window that will connect the greenhouse to the home.

Lay out the site, as described on page 20. Because this model is so light, a simple foundation was chosen: precast concrete piers spaced 4 feet apart. When the concrete blocks are put in place, with 2 inches showing above ground, tie them together with a 2 by 4 redwood sill. (See illustration on page 26.)

The Walls

Constructed in units the walls are nailed to the sill. The back wall is a house wall directly under an overhanging eave. One 2 by 6 ledger board, 12 feet long, is fastened to the house wall with lag screws driven into every other stud. To ensure a waterproof joint between the ledger board and the house, galvanized metal flashing is tucked under the siding and draped over the ledger. The bottom of the ledger board is set at 8 feet high and the front wall at 6 feet.

The front wall of this greenhouse is vertical, but you can angle it as shown for the solar greenhouse on page 91. For a 6-foot-high vertical wall, cut the studs 5 feet 9 inches long; this allows 3 inches for the top and bottom plates. The plates, cut from 2 by 4s, are the horizontal members to which the side wall studs are attached at the top and bottom; the rafters lay across them at the top.

To lay out the front wall, put the top and bottom plates side by side flat on the ground. Mark off every 2 feet, using a framing square to make marks on both plates at the same time. One of the legs of the square is 1½ inches wide, the same as a 2 by 4. Lay it over the center of the mark and pencil in lines on each side.

Lay out the wall with plates and studs in place and then nail them together. Stand on one stud while nailing on the plate to keep the frame from shifting.

Note that the on-center distance between the first stud and the second is only 23¼ inches. The extra ¼ inch will be taken up outside by overlapping one extra ridge when putting on the corrugated plastic panels.

A vent is essential in the front wall, as it is in the roof, to prevent overheating during the summer. You can use a jalousie window, or frame one yourself and cover it with plastic paneling. (See the section on vents on page 30.)

You're now ready to stand up the first wall. With friends helping, place the wall on the foundation and nail and brace it. Use a level to make sure the studs are vertical.

Now you're ready to attach the side walls. These go up essentially as the front wall did.

Marking Plates for Studs

Lay the top and bottom plates side by side; mark O. C. dimensions, in this case every 2'.

Next, center the 1½" leg of a framing square over each mark and draw pencil lines across both plates.

Alternate Door-Wall Layout

This framing allows for a standard (2'6" × 6'8") door. The double rafter on the end of the roof becomes the top plate of the wall.

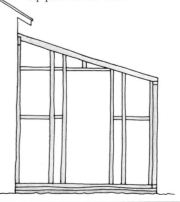

Allowing for the 3½-inch width of the end studs on the front wall, the plates on the 8-foot end walls will be 7 feet 8½ inches long. The studs for the end walls will be 5 feet 9 inches long, the same as the front wall and again 2 feet on center. Cut, mark, and assemble the end wall without the door the same way you did the front wall.

Mark and construct the end wall with the door basically the same way as the other end wall, except leave a space in the center for the width of a 2-foot 6-inch door plus ¼ inch. Frame the opening with studs and then nail in cross braces on each side to keep the wall from shivering every time you close the door.

Note that the door is only 5 feet 9 inches high; you may have to duck a little to go through. The alternate door-wall layout is more difficult to build, but it will accommodate a standard 2-foot 6-inch by 6-foot 8-inch door.

Nail the end walls into place as you did the front wall. Again, use a level to make sure they are vertical.

With both end walls in place, you're ready to raise the roof. The roof will consist of 2 by 4 rafters, 2 feet on center, that will line up with the studs in the front wall. They will be attached with metal joist hangers to the ledger board on the back wall and nailed to the top plate of the front wall.

Start by placing an uncut 2 by 4 rafter over the ledger board and the front wall, and with a pencil mark how the rafter must be cut to fit in the joist hanger and angle down to the front wall. When that rafter is cut and rechecked, use it as a pattern for the other rafters. If you have a vertical front wall 8 feet out from the house, you will have to buy standard 10-foot lengths of 2 by 4s and cut them to fit.

At each end of the roof, put two 2 by 4 rafters together to make a 4 by 4. This makes it easy to nail the vertical pieces that fill in the angle between the top plate on the side wall and the rafters. These pieces are not needed for structural support, but rather for something on which to nail the covering. Put one against the house wall between the top plate and ledger board and one or two others as you see fit.

Next, cut short lengths of 2 by 4s to fill in between the rafters. Nail the narrow part of the 2 by 4 flush with the top of the rafters just at the back edge. The 2 by 4 will form an angle of less than 90 degrees with the top plate.

The Vents

In this greenhouse the vents are essentially frames to hold pieces of plastic paneling that fit between the studs or rafters. The following instructions are for a roof vent. The vent in the front wall is built in the same way but is covered with flat plastic panels to match the wall.

Use 2 by 2s to construct a frame 24 inches long and 22½ inches wide; this will fit exactly between the studs or rafters. Tack redwood corrugated molding or rubber molding on the top and bottom widths and attach a 28-inch length of rigid plastic roofing. The 4-inch overhang in front will prevent leaks.

Since you cannot nail through plastic panels without breaking them, lay them in place and drill holes with a $5/32$-inch bit, 12 inches apart down the rafters. Nail every third ridge on cross braces. The nail for attaching the plastic panels is called a screw nail. It has a waterproofing grommet attached and a wide screw thread, but you hammer it in. The nail should always be put through a ridge in the plastic rather than a gutter to prevent leakage. Don't hammer the nail in too far—just so the head and grommet are snug and secure with the plastic.

From the back of the roof frame, where the vent will hinge, measure down 2 feet and attach a cross brace. The vent frame should fit smoothly into this opening. With it in place, nail quarter-round molding to the rafters and braces right beneath the frame to support it. After the roofing panels are nailed in place with an allowance for the vent opening, install the vent and hinge it to the back plate. Use a hook and eyebolt to keep it from blowing open.

The Roof and Sides

With all the framing done and both vents completed, you are ready to complete the roof and cover the walls.

At the top, along the ledger board, and at the bottom, across the rafters and filler 2 by 4s, nail on corrugated molding. The molding, which follows the same waves as the corrugated plastic panels, prevents drafts. On each rafter place half-round molding strips to support the plastic. If you use rubber or redwood molding, lay a thin bond of sealant on the molding before you nail the plastic panels into place.

Position the panels, leaving a 2-inch overhang in front for water runoff. Cut the panels

to fit flush with the vent opening. Across the front, where there may be strong winds trying to pull the roof loose, drive a screw nail in every ridge for extra insurance.

It is better to cover the walls with flat plastic panels. This makes a tighter fit under the roof line, and flat panels are easier to cut than corrugated ones. Measure and cut the front panels first and nail them in place only after you are sure each panel is square. Lay a bead of sealant over each joint and then cover the joints with strips of redwood or cedar lath.

The Floor

The easiest way to floor a greenhouse is simply to leave the ground bare and use part of it for planting. The problem is that the center walkway generally turns to mud as you water plants and as humidity builds up. You can counter this by laying flagstone, large paving blocks, or round concrete pads available at garden supply centers.

Many greenhouse owners prefer a floor consisting of 3 to 4 inches of gravel or crushed stone. This type of floor is not only inexpensive

A concrete floor should be sloped toward drains leading outside.

A brick-and-stone floor is inexpensive to lay, functional, and easy to maintain.

One of the most attractive and practical floors is brick on sand. This works equally well for a small freestanding greenhouse or a large extension off the house. In addition to letting water and fine grit disappear through the floor, bricks will catch and hold solar heat during the day and release it back into the greenhouse at night for added warmth. Black bricks will absorb more heat. When planning the floor, figure on 3½ bricks per square feet of floor area.

After you've finished framing and glazing the greenhouse, lay down a 3-inch layer of sand. You may have to excavate so that the finished floor is not above the door sill.

Rather than bricking the entire floor, you may choose to lay a brick walkway between 2 by 4s down the center of the greenhouse and spread gravel for the rest of the floor.

After distributing the sand evenly on the greenhouse floor, dampen it thoroughly to settle it. Kneeling on a piece of plywood to keep from digging up the sand, level a section along the back wall with a 2 by 4. Start laying the bricks in one corner and keep working out from there. If you have benches down only one side, start opposite them so that any cut bricks will be under the benches.

Set the bricks as snugly as you can against each other. There will still be about a ⅛-inch gap. Later these gaps will be filled in with sand. As you lay the bricks, check your progress with a level. After you finish a section, lay a 2 by 4 along a row of bricks and hammer it firmly to set and level the bricks.

Bricks do not break cleanly—a frustrating matter when you try to fit them into leftover spaces against the walls. You may want to rent a masonry saw for a clean cut. Otherwise, score the brick first with a cold chisel and then make a single sharp cut. If you feel the edges are too uneven, hide them by laying a 2 by 2 baseboard of redwood or other rot-resistant lumber along the perimeter.

After the bricks are laid, cover them with a layer of sand. Leave the sand on the bricks for a couple of days as you walk around on it. The floor will soon be as tight and firm as if it had been mortared. Use a broom to sweep the sand back and forth until all the cracks are filled.

Although the bricks used in a solarium are sometimes waxed for a finished appearance, in a greenhouse they should remain unwaxed and porous.

and easy to install, but it also keeps the mud away. You can water freely in the greenhouse and let the water run into the gravel or crushed stones where it will help increase humidity and discourage slugs and snails.

Some greenhouse owners build a poured concrete slab contoured toward drainage holes leading outdoors. This type of floor can be hosed regularly, and it helps cut down on diseases that may breed in damp open soil areas.

Other greenhouse hobbyists consider a concrete floor too expensive and bothersome to maintain. Instead of having a floor that must be cleaned regularly, they prefer one in which excess water and fine dirt take care of themselves by working back into the ground.

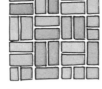

Brick Patterns

Traditional

Herringbone

Jack-on-jack

Basket weave

Half basket weave

Angled herringbone

Top: The brick must be cut to fit the allotted space in the floor.
Center left: First score the brick with a cold chisel. Tap the chisel lightly with a hammer.
Center right: Break the brick with a single sharp blow.
Bottom left: Tap the cut brick into place with a mallet.
Bottom right: Shovel sand onto the floor and sweep it into the cracks with a broom.

Gothic Arch Greenhouse

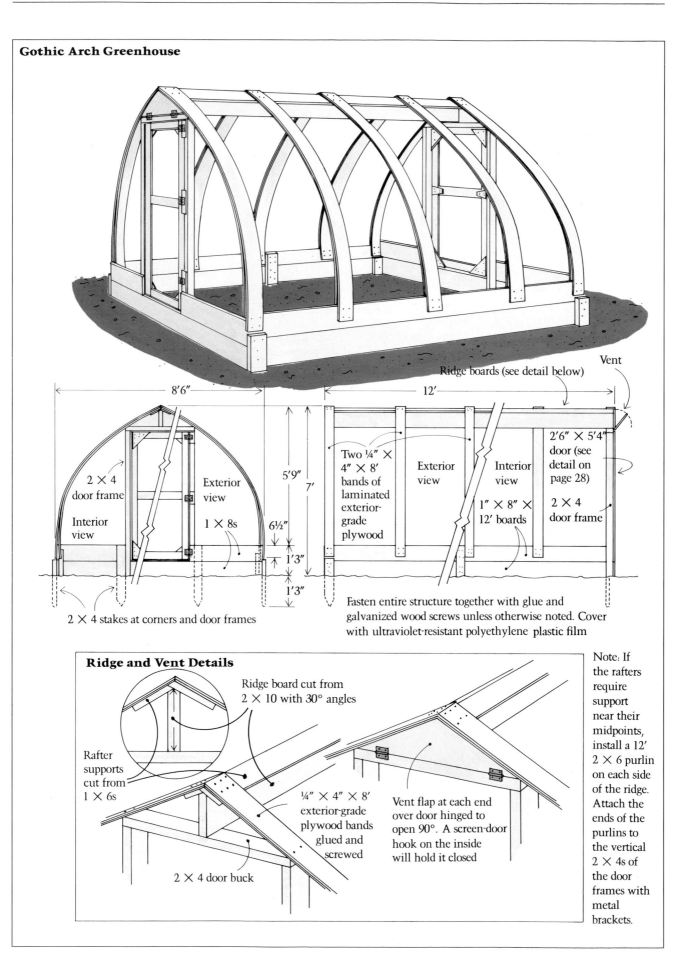

8′6″

12′

Ridge boards (see detail below)

Vent

5′9″

7′

6½″

1′3″

1′3″

2 × 4 door frame

Interior view

Exterior view

1 × 8s

2 × 4 stakes at corners and door frames

Two ¼″ × 4″ × 8′ bands of laminated exterior-grade plywood

Exterior view

Interior view

1″ × 8″ × 12′ boards

2′6″ × 5′4″ door (see detail on page 28)

2 × 4 door frame

Fasten entire structure together with glue and galvanized wood screws unless otherwise noted. Cover with ultraviolet-resistant polyethylene plastic film

Ridge and Vent Details

Ridge board cut from 2 × 10 with 30° angles

Rafter supports cut from 1 × 6s

¼″ × 4″ × 8′ exterior-grade plywood bands glued and screwed

Vent flap at each end over door hinged to open 90°. A screen-door hook on the inside will hold it closed

2 × 4 door buck

Note: If the rafters require support near their midpoints, install a 12′ 2 × 6 purlin on each side of the ridge. Attach the ends of the purlins to the vertical 2 × 4s of the door frames with metal brackets.

GOTHIC ARCH GREENHOUSE

Although designed to be lightweight and portable, this gothic arch greenhouse could also be placed on a conventional foundation for more permanence. It can be covered with polyethylene film plastic or, for more durability, with flat rigid plastic panels.

Using 1 by 8s stacked two high and cleated together, make a frame measuring 12 feet long and 8 feet 6 inches wide. For the roof supports, cut 20 strips, each 4 inches wide and 8 feet long, from ¼-inch exterior-grade plywood. Glue and nail them together in twos so that you end up with 10 bands. Leave the bottom 8 inches unglued and unnailed.

The next step is to frame the end support walls and the doors. At each end, cut an opening 2 feet 9 inches wide in the center of the top board of the frame.

Notch two 6-foot lengths of 2 by 4 to fit flush with the bottom board of the frame. Nail on a 2-foot 9-inch door buck at the top and then nail each door frame into position.

For the ridge board, cut a 30-degree angle on each side of a 12-foot length of 2 by 10 and toenail it in place on the center of the door buck. To each side of the ridge board, nail a 1 by 6, 12 feet long. This forms the support for the bands of plywood rafters.

Attach the rafters to the ridge line with galvanized wood screws, and nail and glue them to the frame. Start at one end with the band nailed and glued on the inside only. Curve it over the door frame and nail it there before screwing it into the ridge boards. Now nail and glue the outside flap to the frame. Complete both ends and then finish at the middle supports.

Cut pieces of ⅜-inch exterior-grade plywood to fit the gable openings above the doors. Attach them with hinges so they can be opened for added ventilation.

The doors are made from 2 by 2s with one cross brace at the center. Triangular plywood braces, or gussets, at each corner give added strength. The doors should swing out to save space, and they should be hinged so they will not open in the direction of the prevailing wind.

Complete the greenhouse by covering it with flat plastic panels or with film plastic that is resistant to damage from ultraviolet rays. Refer to page 31 for information on flooring the greenhouse.

In windy areas anchor the greenhouse to the ground. After setting the greenhouse in desired location, drive two stakes 18 inches into the ground on each side of the door and two on each side of the framework. Fasten the stakes to the frame with wood screws.

The curved walls of the gothic arch greenhouse shed heavy snow and rain, and they let in abundant sunlight. Plants like these cactus and succulents can be grown the year around, as long as the greenhouse is properly ventilated in summer and adequately heated in winter.

A-frame Greenhouse

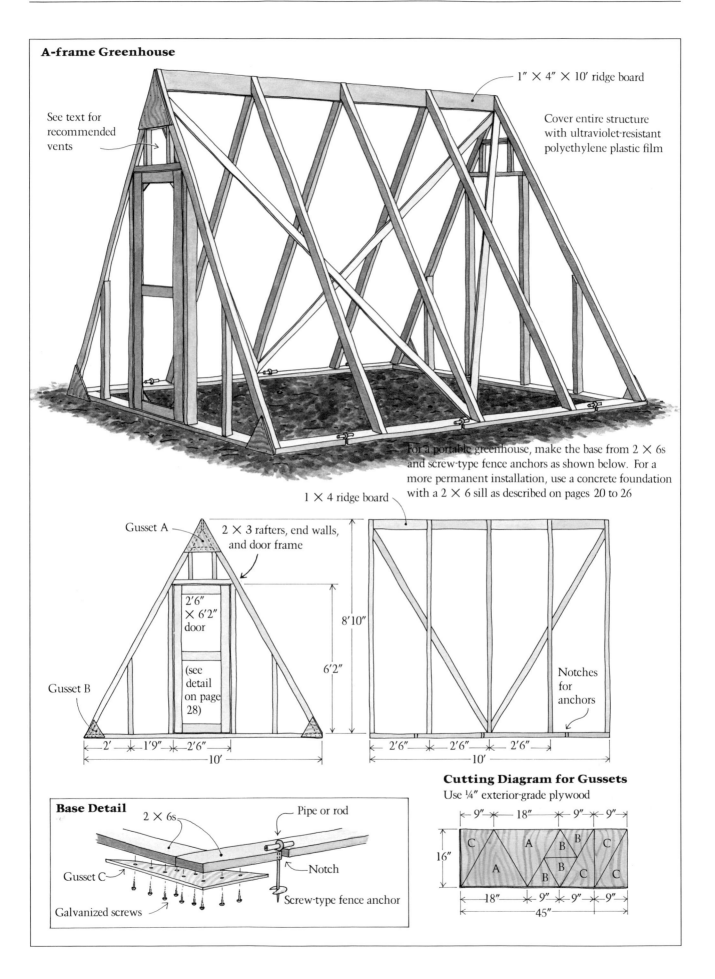

$1'' \times 4'' \times 10'$ ridge board

See text for recommended vents

Cover entire structure with ultraviolet-resistant polyethylene plastic film

For a portable greenhouse, make the base from 2×6s and screw-type fence anchors as shown below. For a more permanent installation, use a concrete foundation with a 2×6 sill as described on pages 20 to 26

1×4 ridge board

Gusset A

2×3 rafters, end walls, and door frame

$2'6'' \times 6'2''$ door

(see detail on page 28)

Gusset B

$8'10''$

$6'2''$

$2'$ — $1'9''$ — $2'6''$

$10'$

Notches for anchors

$2'6''$ — $2'6''$ — $2'6''$

$10'$

Base Detail

2×6s

Pipe or rod

Gusset C

Notch

Galvanized screws

Screw-type fence anchor

Cutting Diagram for Gussets

Use ¼" exterior-grade plywood

— 9" — 18" — 9" — 9" —

16"

C   A   B B   C

A   B   C   C

— 18" — 9" — 9" — 9" —

45"

A-FRAME GREENHOUSE

The chief advantage of the A-frame lies in its easy construction. Also, the steep roof sheds snow efficiently. This model is relatively small and lightweight; it can be considered portable, although several strong people are needed to move it. For more permanence, the greenhouse can be placed on a conventional foundation.

The greenhouse sits on a 10- by 10-foot base. You will need four 2 by 6s, 10 feet long, to construct this bottom support. Fifteen 2 by 3s, 10 feet long, are needed for the rafters and end walls. (If 2 by 3s are not available, you can substitute 2 by 4s.) The ridge board and door are made from 1 by 4s.

Assemble the frame, using precut plywood gussets at the corners. Cut one rafter to fit at the proper angle and use it as the pattern for the other nine rafters. Build one wall with the 1 by 4 ridge board nailed to it, then stand and brace that wall in place. Then nail the

other five rafters in place. With the whole structure still braced, nail the diagonal braces. Finish the end walls.

To provide proper venting, frame in a 10-inch diameter fan above the door and a louvered opening of the same size at the opposite end of the greenhouse.

This model is covered on the outside with 8-mil film plastic resistant to ultraviolet rays. For additional protection—essential in cold areas—put another layer of ordinary 4-mil polyethylene inside. Leave a space between the two to create a thermal barrier.

Securely anchor the greenhouse to the ground. One method is to use a screw-type fence anchor set into notches cut in the base and held with short pieces of reinforcing rod, or rebar, pushed through the screw eye. See page 31 for information on constructing a floor for the greenhouse.

The shape of the A-frame greenhouse limits the kinds of plants that may be grown in it. Tall shrubs and other plants requiring ample head room are not suitable. These cymbidium orchids do nicely in an A-frame structure.

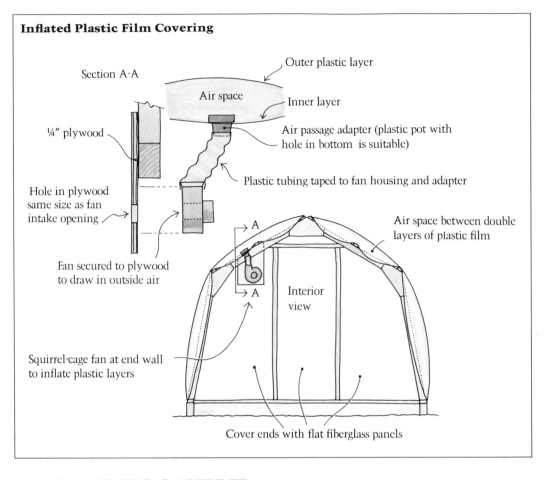

Inflated Plastic Film Covering

Section A-A

Outer plastic layer

Air space

Inner layer

¼″ plywood

Air passage adapter (plastic pot with hole in bottom is suitable)

Plastic tubing taped to fan housing and adapter

Hole in plywood same size as fan intake opening

Air space between double layers of plastic film

A

Fan secured to plywood to draw in outside air

A

Interior view

Squirrel-cage fan at end wall to inflate plastic layers

Cover ends with flat fiberglass panels

FREESTANDING GAMBREL ROOF GREENHOUSE

Built similarly to a barn, the freestanding gambrel roof greenhouse has considerable structural strength and is excellent in regions with heavy snowfall. Erected in sections, it lends itself readily to either a film plastic or rigid plastic covering.

One of the most time-consuming aspects of building this type of greenhouse is cutting the plywood gussets. To speed this process, cut one of each pattern as shown in the diagram on the opposite page, and use it as a pattern for all the others. Also carefully note the cutting diagram for the legs and rafters. After they are all cut, glue and nail the legs and rafters together with the gussets.

For a 10- by 12-foot greenhouse, the frame is constructed by sinking 4 by 4s, 4 feet long, into the ground. Leave enough of the post exposed so that you can nail on the 1 by 12 frame. (This greenhouse can be placed on a traditional foundation for more permanence.)

To level the posts, drive them in about 30 inches and cut off the excess after you have put the frame in place and adjusted it until it is level. Place the posts 6 feet apart down the sides and 5 feet apart across the front and back. Across the top of the 4 by 4 posts goes a 2 by 4 sill. Mark the sill where each leg and end support will go.

To frame the greenhouse, put the preconstructed end walls in place first and brace them securely. Put the two 1 by 4 purlins on the ridge, then put in the two center supports and hold them in place by nailing them to the purlins. Double-check that everything is square before nailing. The structure is further strengthened with 1 by 4 purlins at the middle and lower edge of the roof.

As an alternative to rigid plastic, two layers of film plastic can be used for glazing. You can maintain the thermal layer of air between them with a small squirrel-cage fan. Install the fan at one end near the ridge line by mounting it to a plywood panel suspended from the end rafter. Cut a hole in the plywood for the fan to draw in air, and use flexible plastic tubing and a plastic pot with a hole cut in the bottom to direct the air between the two layers of plastic.

Use techniques discussed on page 31 to construct a floor for the greenhouse.

Gambrel Roof Greenhouse

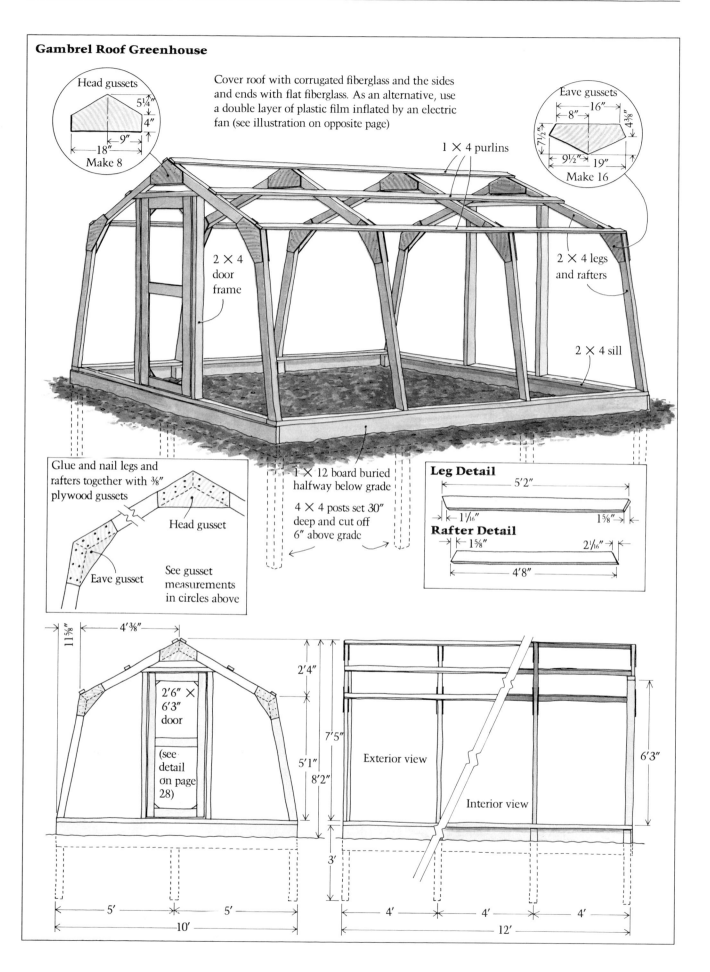

Head gussets
Make 8

5¼"
4"
9"
18"

Cover roof with corrugated fiberglass and the sides and ends with flat fiberglass. As an alternative, use a double layer of plastic film inflated by an electric fan (see illustration on opposite page)

Eave gussets
16"
8"
4⅜"
7½"
9½"
19"
Make 16

1 × 4 purlins

2 × 4 legs and rafters

2 × 4 door frame

2 × 4 legs and rafters

2 × 4 sill

Glue and nail legs and rafters together with ⅜" plywood gussets

Head gusset

Eave gusset

See gusset measurements in circles above

1 × 12 board buried halfway below grade

4 × 4 posts set 30" deep and cut off 6" above grade

Leg Detail
5'2"
1¹/₁₆"
1⅝"

Rafter Detail
1⅝"
2¹/₁₆"
4'8"

11⅝"
4'⅜"

2'6" × 6'3" door

(see detail on page 28)

2'4"

7'5"

5'1"

8'2"

Exterior view

Interior view

6'3"

3'

5'
5'
10'

4'
4'
4'
12'

SIMPLIFIED GAMBREL ROOF GREENHOUSE

A simpler version of the freestanding gambrel roof greenhouse, this design does not use gussets. The key to building this lightweight, 8- by 12-foot greenhouse is finding and cutting the proper angles for the roof.

If you live in a dry climate, the greenhouse can go directly on the ground, although it is better to place it on a conventional foundation. Once the sill is in place, build the two side walls, making them 4 feet 10 inches high so that a 5-foot length of rigid plastic siding will completely cover the bottom sill.

Find the angles for the rafters with a sheet of 4 by 8 plywood. (The 8 feet represent the width of the greenhouse.) Draw a line down the center of the plywood sheet dividing it into two equal squares. Set two lengths of 2 by 4, each about 4 feet long, at the desired angle on the plywood and trace the outline. Connect the intersections, as shown on the opposite page, to find the angles. Use cut rafters to diagram the other side of the plywood.

Once all the rafter legs have been measured and cut, nail one 1 by 4 at the top and bottom of them just as if you were constructing a wall on the ground. When you're finished, you'll have four roof sections. Place both lower sections on top of the wall and brace them temporarily in place. To tie them together and support them, run a cross brace between each one at the top. Now, put the two top components in place and nail them. The end walls are made with 2 by 4s under each roof angle and under the center.

A door can be cut to fit from 1 by 4s and a vent positioned above the door. As with the freestanding gambrel roof, this greenhouse can be covered with rigid panels or inflated film plastic.

If the greenhouse is not built on a foundation, anchor it by drilling holes every 4 feet through the bottom plate and sill and by driving 3-foot lengths of reinforcing rod, or rebar, into the ground through the holes. Bend the top 2 inches at a 90-degree angle.

A floor will complete the greenhouse; see page 31 for information on putting in a floor.

A simplified gambrel roof allows ample head room for tall plants and hanging pots. Here, a collection of orchids fills the greenhouse.

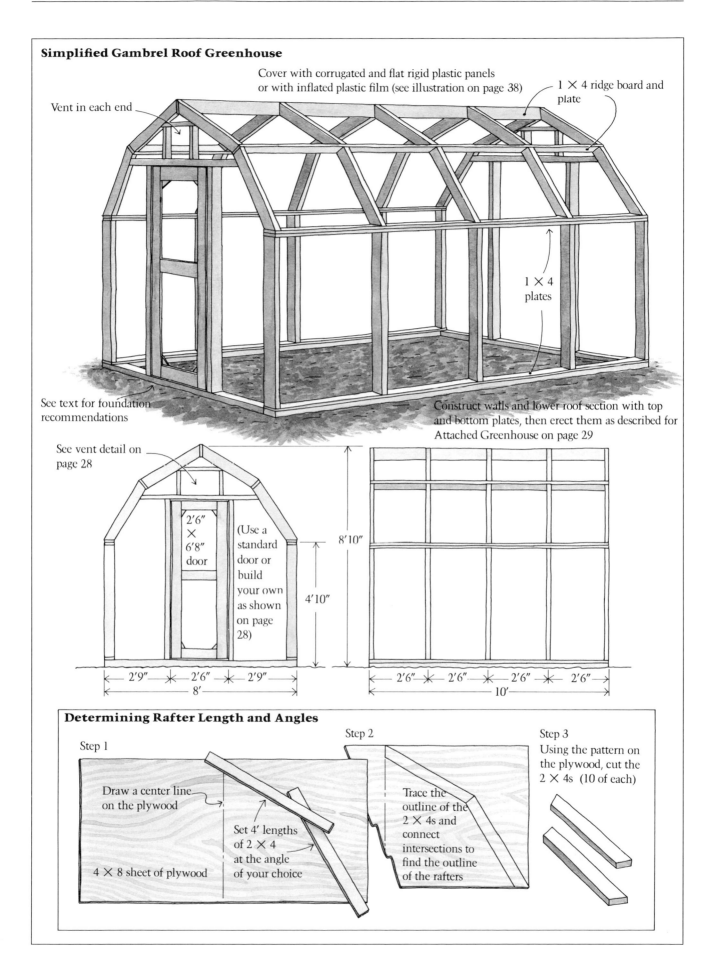

Simplified Gambrel Roof Greenhouse

Cover with corrugated and flat rigid plastic panels
or with inflated plastic film (see illustration on page 38)

1 × 4 ridge board and plate

Vent in each end

1 × 4 plates

See text for foundation recommendations

Construct walls and lower roof section with top and bottom plates, then erect them as described for Attached Greenhouse on page 29

See vent detail on page 28

2'6" × 6'8" door

(Use a standard door or build your own as shown on page 28)

8'10"

4'10"

2'9" 2'6" 2'9"
8'

2'6" 2'6" 2'6" 2'6"
10'

Determining Rafter Length and Angles

Step 1

Draw a center line on the plywood

Set 4' lengths of 2 × 4 at the angle of your choice

4 × 8 sheet of plywood

Step 2

Trace the outline of the 2 × 4s and connect intersections to find the outline of the rafters

Step 3
Using the pattern on the plywood, cut the 2 × 4s (10 of each)

Snow-Country Greenhouse

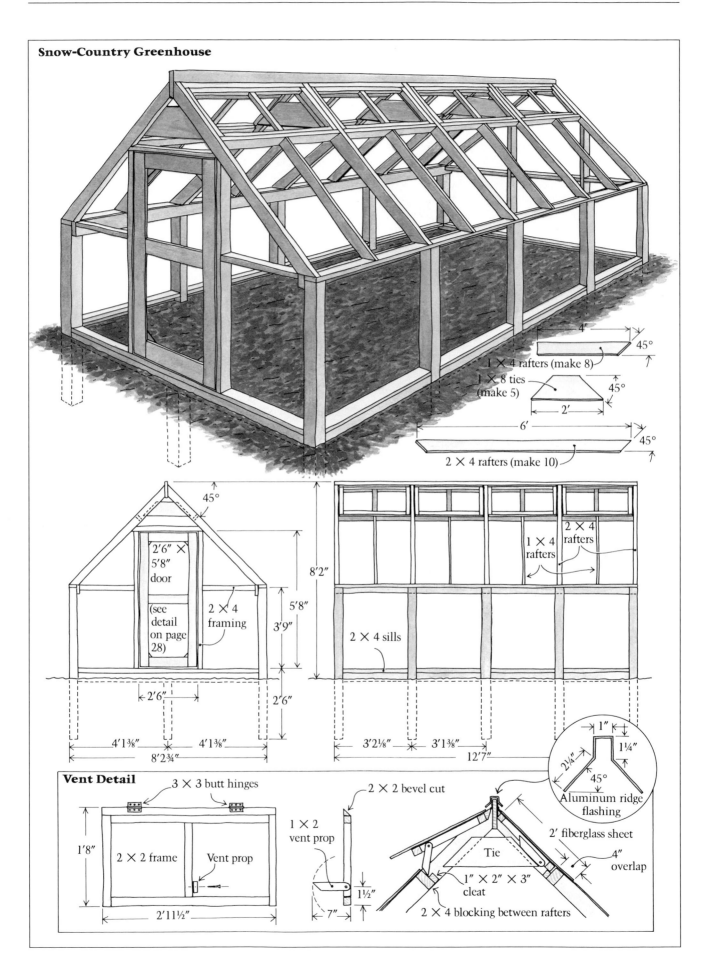

4'

45°

1 × 4 rafters (make 8)

1 × 8 ties
(make 5)

2'

45°

6'

2 × 4 rafters (make 10)

45°

45°

45°

2'6" ×
5'8"
door

(see
detail
on page
28)

2 × 4
framing

8'2"

5'8"

3'9"

2'6"

2'6"

4'1⅜"   4'1⅜"

8'2¾"

2 × 4
rafters

1 × 4
rafters

2 × 4 sills

3'2⅛"   3'1⅜"

12'7"

1"

1¼"

2¼"

45°

Aluminum ridge
flashing

Vent Detail

3 × 3 butt hinges

2 × 2 bevel cut

1 × 2
vent prop

1'8"

2 × 2 frame   Vent prop

2'11½"

1½"

7"

Tie

1" × 2" × 3"
cleat

2 × 4 blocking between rafters

2' fiberglass sheet

4"
overlap

In addition to roof vents, other methods are used to cool the greenhouse during hot summers. Here, vines help shade the interior of the structure.

SNOW-COUNTRY GREENHOUSE

The plan for this greenhouse, designed by the University of Connecticut, features a steep A-frame roof for shedding snow quickly. The continuous line of roof vents provides natural cooling in the summer.

Sink ten 4 by 4 posts about 2½ feet in the ground, with 3 feet 9 inches remaining above the surface. To get these exact measurements, first sink the posts and then use a line level before cutting the tops at the required height. For the rafters to fit smoothly, the posts must be set 8 feet 3¾ inches apart.

After the posts are in place, place the 2 by 4 continuous top plate all the way around on top of the posts and nail it in. Next, put on the 2 by 4 side plate, which helps support the rafter ends. You will need ten 2 by 4 rafters, 6 feet long, and eight 1 by 4 rafters, 4 feet long. Cut a 45-degree angle at both ends of the ten long rafters and a 45-degree angle at the bottom end only of the eight short rafters.

Frame the doors at both ends, and use the framing to support the end rafters. After nailing the end rafters to the 1 by 8 ridge board, put up the other rafters, spaced 3 feet 1⅜ inches on center.

Use 2 by 4 blocking to frame the vent openings. Then center the 1 by 4 rafters on the blocking and toenail them in. Frame the vents with 2 by 2s cut according to the illustration on the opposite page to fit between each rafter.

Cover the greenhouse with rigid plastic and add aluminum flashing on the ridge. A floor (see page 31) will complete the greenhouse.

Buying and Assembling a Kit

Instead of building from scratch, you may choose to erect a greenhouse from a kit. Prefabricated models are available in many different styles, sizes, and materials.

For the greenhouse fancier who doesn't have the time or skills to build from scratch and doesn't want to hire a professional builder, there is an alternative: buying and assembling a prefabricated greenhouse from a kit. Today, there is a wide range of greenhouse packages containing everything from structural components to nuts and bolts. Prefabricated models vary in size from modest structures not much bigger than a cold frame to full-sized working greenhouses. All include complete, step-by-step directions for assembly, and most require only basic tools such as a screwdriver, hammer, and staple gun.

The cost of a kit is usually midway between that of a greenhouse you build from a plan and a custom-designed, professionally constructed greenhouse. Most models are priced between $150 and $5,000. Even with limited building skills, you and a friend or two can put together a good-quality greenhouse in anywhere from a few hours to a weekend or two.

Having the greenhouse kit entirely installed by a contractor is a possibility that should be considered from the very beginning, especially in the case of an elaborate kit. Many kit manufacturers have franchised dealers who offer installation services. They already know the company's products and can usually be counted on to do a good job. Your final cost will still be considerably less than for a custom-built structure.

Purchased greenhouses range from simple to lavish. This elaborate glass structure sits on a weathered brick foundation that blends with the brick house to which the greenhouse is attached.

This Salem, Oregon, gardener starts vegetable seedlings in a temporary tunnel-type greenhouse set up in his vegetable patch. The sides of the greenhouse roll up for ventilation.

RESEARCHING GREENHOUSE KITS

Today, greenhouse manufacturers offer a tremendous choice of products, from traditional wood and glass structures to plastic-covered geodesic domes and from portable greenhouses designed to extend the growing season to permanent home additions. Just about any type of greenhouse imaginable is available in kit form.

Before deciding on the type of structure best suited to your needs, you must do a fair amount of research. Most greenhouse suppliers offer several types of kits and an almost unlimited number of options, including choices in size and in framing materials and coverings. You can even have special modifications built right into a kit. Since kits—even ones that look similar—can vary widely in price and quality, it pays to check around carefully before committing yourself.

Gather all the pertinent information and read it over carefully several times before deciding just what kind of kit you want and how you plan to install it. Luckily, there are many helpful sources of information.

Looking at Mail Order Catalogs

Greenhouse suppliers produce catalogs that range in quality from simple photocopied sheets listing the features of a single model to elaborate full-color brochures describing dozens of models. Begin your research by contacting some of the greenhouse sources listed on page 57. The Hobby Greenhouse Association, the address of which is included on the same page, can supply you with a lengthier list of sources on request.

As you study the catalogs, keep a close eye on prices. Remember that a major disparity in cost between two models that look alike usually means a difference in the quality and longevity of materials or in the ease of construction. A greenhouse offering better access, more efficient ventilation, and superior insulation will cost more than a lower-quality model that appears similar.

Checking the Yellow Pages

The usefulness of your local telephone directory will depend on how important the hobby greenhouse industry is in your area. Listings under *Greenhouses* or *Greenhouses and*

Solariums in some areas may consist mostly of specialists in large-scale commercial greenhouses. In other areas, especially large urban centers, the listings may concentrate on costly home additions rather than do-it-yourself kits.

Whether or not local greenhouse sources carry the kind of product you are seeking, they can offer advice about the best kinds of structures and coverings for your climate. No one knows the effects of local climatic conditions on greenhouses better than someone dealing with greenhouse growers on a daily basis. Compile a list of questions before you call.

If you are interested in a model the company sells, ask the sales representative for the names of some satisfied customers in the area. In talking to these greenhouse owners, ask why they chose that particular model and if they are satisfied with it. If possible, go out and see some of the greenhouses in operation.

Visiting Showrooms

Large greenhouse companies usually display their products in showrooms. If there are any in your area, by all means visit them. Make an appointment so that a knowledgeable sales representative will be on hand to answer questions. Even if you decide to buy elsewhere, you will probably pick up some useful information.

Attending Home and Garden Shows

Greenhouse suppliers often participate in home and garden shows and agricultural fairs. Most of the companies provide helpful brochures, and some may even display greenhouses. You may be offered a special discount if you buy a greenhouse during the event. Before committing to a purchase, make sure the product meets your needs; even at special rates, an inappropriate product won't bring satisfaction.

Since their hilly property offers no level site for a greenhouse, the owners set up this prefabricated model on a cliff-side deck overlooking a spectacular panorama.

This freestanding gambrel-style kit greenhouse is perched on a deck adjacent to the house.

Contacting Plant Societies

Local plant societies may be the best place to obtain information about greenhouse kits from the point of view of hobby growers. Ask if you can talk to members who have gone through the experience of buying and assembling a greenhouse kit. You'll likely get valuable information and suggestions that would otherwise have taken months to collect. Learning from other people's mistakes is far better than having to learn from your own.

Reading Publications

Look for information on greenhouse kits in gardening publications. *Hobby Greenhouse* is a magazine devoted to the subject. Published by the Hobby Greenhouse Association, it contains articles describing amateur growers' personal experiences with greenhouses of all kinds. The publication also includes advertisements for greenhouse kits. For a subscription write to *Hobby Greenhouse*, 8 Glen Terrace, Bedford, MA 01730.

CHOOSING A KIT

After studying the information you've gathered, you must begin to make some decisions about the type of structure you want. Practical considerations may help to narrow the choices. For example, if you plan to assemble the greenhouse on your own with the help of a friend, you may opt for a simply designed, lightly framed kit. Or, if your dream greenhouse turns out to be beyond your budget, you may find yourself considering a similar structure that is smaller or offers fewer features. However, don't compromise so much that you buy a product that doesn't meet your needs.

Evaluating Ease of Assembly

Depending on your skills and available time, the amount of work involved in assembling the greenhouse may be a deciding factor in choosing a kit. Although most kits come with all structural components except the foundation, a few inexpensive models require that you supply some parts. In these cases, complete instructions are provided, and usually minimal carpentry skills are needed. Even when the cost of the extra parts is included, this type of kit is almost always less expensive than a model requiring only assembly.

Even in kits that supply all parts, there are differences in the ease of assembly. In many top-of-the-line kits, all structural components are predrilled, and the panels are cut to size or even preassembled. You just fit parts together and screw them in place. In less expensive models, you may find yourself cutting panels and making minor adjustments to the structure itself. Since predrilled structures and preassembled panels are considerably easier and faster to install, you may judge the extra cost worthwhile, especially if your carpentry skills are limited. Check with the supplier to determine exactly what work is involved in assembly, because this is not always clearly stated in a catalog or brochure.

Deciding on Freestanding Versus Attached

Unless you intend to call in expert help, you are usually better off with a freestanding greenhouse. Every aspect of installing an attached model is more critical, because the structure is an extension of the house. The sealing must be perfect, especially if you plan to keep a connecting doorway open at times. The foundation must be deep and solidly constructed, particularly in cold-winter climates; otherwise, uneven freezing and thawing around the house can tilt the greenhouse and cause glass or rigid plastic panels to crack. The house wall may also require certain modifications beyond your skills—for example, you may have to deal with a roof overhang or work around an awkwardly placed window or door.

An attached greenhouse should be in keeping with the style of your home, or it may reduce the value of your property and provoke the ire of the local building department—if, indeed, the local authority permits the structure to be built. This is not to say that you should not consider an attached greenhouse kit, but be prepared to encounter more obstacles than you would with a freestanding model.

On the positive side, an attached greenhouse requires less material than a freestanding structure and thus is often considerably cheaper and faster to install. Also, extending

water and electricity to an attached unit is easier than running lines to a freestanding structure in the backyard.

Although a freestanding greenhouse is less accessible from the house, it offers many advantages. A simple foundation is sufficient for lightweight models. The greenhouse can be placed where it doesn't dominate the landscape, and its appearance has less influence on the overall look of the home. It is easier to add extensions to freestanding than to attached units. This allows newcomers to greenhouse growing to save money by starting off with a smaller unit that can be expanded.

Planning for Expansion

Unless you choose an attached model designed to meet your space requirements exactly, it is wise to consider a model that offers some possibility of expansion. First-time greenhouse owners almost invariably find their structures too small after a few years of growing experience.

This prefabricated model is attached to the house. Decking was built around the greenhouse; the greenhouse itself has a brick floor.

Fortunately, most hobby kits are designed with expansion in mind.

An extension module, usually available in 3- or 4-foot lengths, can easily be inserted in a functioning greenhouse by removing one of the gable ends, installing the new section, and replacing the end. The greatest effort usually occurs in extending the foundation, not in installing the module.

Instead of expanding, you may decide to start off with a seasonal greenhouse (see page 53) or a structure of lower quality than the final greenhouse desired. An inexpensive used greenhouse (see page 52) is another option. Later you can sell your temporary greenhouse and reinvest in a larger, more permanent structure.

Deciding on the Covering

Many types of covering are available in greenhouse kits, and there is little reason to recommend one over the other. Read pages 14 to 16 carefully, and let your needs determine the best product for you.

Novice builders may do well to avoid glass as a covering. Not only does glass require a more solid foundation than plastic, but it is heavier, harder to handle, and more easily broken. If you really want glass, think about hiring an experienced contractor for the installation.

Although attaching film plastic may seem easy, many people find it difficult to make the plastic taut. Read the supplier's instructions carefully, and schedule at least one practice run before actually tacking it into place. A videotape demonstration is useful. If you bought the kit locally, ask the retailer to show you how it's done.

Getting Sample Plans

After you've narrowed your choice to two or three kits, ask the suppliers for sample plans. Most will gladly agree.

Previewing the plans can be important, because some prefabricated greenhouses are more complicated to install than others. Unless you know what to expect, you may find yourself in over your head and having to call a contractor to finish the job—an unplanned move that can send costs skyrocketing.

After carefully studying several plans, you may find one that meets your skill level. It is also possible that the type of greenhouse you want is too complicated for you to assemble on your own. For example, permanent models with glass panels are often best left to experts. If you know ahead of time that outside help is needed, then you'll be able to factor in the added cost and take your time in selecting a suitable contractor.

Roll-up shades help cool this attached glass greenhouse during the hottest summer months.

Obtaining Accessories

Generally, accessories are not included in a greenhouse kit, although they may be available as options. Wiring, lighting, plumbing, heating, ventilation, benches, and irrigation systems must be added at your own expense. Most greenhouse kits are designed so that benches, wall-mounted shelves, and hanging baskets can be added without any major modifications to the structure itself.

Consider dealing with a greenhouse supplier who also offers a good line of accessories. Although less expensive accessories may be available locally, it is often a good idea to buy them from the supplier at the same time you purchase the greenhouse. That way, you can be sure that the accessories are intended for greenhouse use and that they are appropriate for the structure you've chosen.

Another advantage in buying accessories such as fans and a heating system directly from the greenhouse supplier is that you will save money on delivery costs if the entire package comes from the same source at the same time. Remember, too, that using the wrong kind of equipment in the greenhouse may result in damage that invalidates the guarantee. When you install a recommended accessory according to the supplier's instructions, there is virtually no chance of that happening.

Evaluating Support

Before making a final decision, you may want to consider the type of guarantees you will get and the level of technical assistance available.

Guarantees   Although your purchase will be based mainly on personal preference, quality, and price, don't overlook the guarantees when making a final decision. Many greenhouse kits offer a five-year warranty on material defects and workmanship, plus a separate guarantee on the greenhouse covering. Depending on the type of covering, this guarantee will vary from a year or two for some types of greenhouse film to as many as ten years for more durable materials. If you're looking for a trouble-free greenhouse, choose a covering with a long, thorough guarantee. Accessories, such as heaters, fans, and vent openers, are usually guaranteed separately by their manufacturers.

Beware of any product with a much weaker guarantee than others in its category. It may mean that the product is constructed of inferior materials, and it signifies the manufacturer's lack of confidence in the product.

Technical assistance   Usually, technical assistance is readily available through the manufacturer or the distributor. Avoid long, complicated searches at the last minute by

Left: Accessories such as greenhouse fans must be purchased separately.
Right: Usually, the manufacturer provides a separate guarantee for the greenhouse covering. Protect your investment by using a noncorrosive shading material on the panels.

This attached greenhouse is erected on a stone foundation identical to the house facade.

knowing in advance who is responsible for answering questions.

The latest, and perhaps the most practical, innovation in technical assistance is the installation video. Offered by an increasing number of companies, it is worth watching twice: once before you begin and then as you proceed with the installation. Although not usually included in the basic cost of the greenhouse, an installation video is well worth buying.

Determining the Total Cost

In the end, you will decide to purchase a particular kit only if the final cost is acceptable. Be sure to calculate all costs, not just the price of the kit itself. If you decide to hire professional help, add the labor costs; a few calls to local contractors will give a reasonable estimate. You must also consider shipping costs, which can range from approximately $30 for a small, portable structure to more than $300 for a large, permanent greenhouse. Unless you are able to pick up the kit from the manufacturer, there is no way to save money on transport. Even buying from a local retail outlet is no solution: Shipping has already been added to the bill.

If you find that the greenhouse you really want is beyond your budget, there are ways of cutting corners. Unfortunately, most of these are stopgap measures. For example, poorer materials usually mean increased maintenance and more frequent replacement, so the initial savings are eaten up in the long run. A better way of saving money is to do more of the work yourself. Some manufacturers charge less if you are willing to drill the holes and cut and assemble the panels.

Used Greenhouses

Secondhand structures can be a real bargain, especially if they are relatively new. Moving them is rarely a problem, as most kits that are designed for easy installation are also easy to take apart. If the plans are no longer available, label all the parts so that there is no confusion when you reassemble them. Although some small structures may be light enough to move intact, it is better to take them apart to avoid accidental damage in the move.

Before buying a used greenhouse, check the structural components for signs of damage or fatigue. The structure should be stable and the covering relatively airtight. Make sure that replacement parts are still available. Don't be surprised if the covering needs partial or complete replacement; the latest film coverings and rigid plastic panels are much more durable than those used on greenhouses only a few years ago. If a new cover is required, add it to the purchase price.

One of the negative aspects of a used greenhouse is that it is very rarely exactly what you want. On the other hand, the purchase may be worthwhile if the price is right and the structure can be adapted to your needs. Many hobbyists use a secondhand greenhouse as a stopgap until they can afford to buy the structure they want.

Used hobby greenhouses can be difficult to find. Plant societies or local greenhouse retailers may be able to direct you to someone who is replacing a smaller structure with a new, larger one. Someone wishing to sell a greenhouse may advertise in the local paper, or you can place an ad looking for a seller. A new homeowner who inherits the previous owner's greenhouse and doesn't know what to do with it may be only too happy to respond to such an ad.

Seasonal Greenhouses

Often, prospective owners assume that all greenhouses are permanent structures designed for use throughout the year. If your needs are seasonal and you are deterred by the high cost of a permanent structure, don't automatically reject the idea of a greenhouse. A temporary or portable greenhouse may serve you well.

Few greenhouses are marketed as temporary structures, but many of the less expensive kits will do nicely if used that way. Among these are the tunnel-type, or hoop-style, greenhouses. Little more than a transparent plastic tent stretched over a wood, aluminum, steel, or PVC frame, the greenhouse can be installed in only a few hours. Although the greenhouse will last longer if placed on a foundation, it can sit directly on the ground. Until recently, the usual covering was an inexpensive film plastic that required frequent replacement. Now, many models come with film plastic guaranteed for at least five years.

The disadvantages of a tunnel-type greenhouse are poor insulation and inadequate ventilation. Generally, only one layer of film plastic is supplied, although a second layer can be added and air pumped between the two (see page 38). Ventilating the greenhouse usually requires opening doors or rolling up the sides during hot weather. But in spring and fall, when the sun heats the greenhouse and the days aren't long enough for excess heat to build up inside, tunnel-type greenhouses work very efficiently.

Extending the Growing Season
Typically, hobby growers use a seasonal greenhouse as an intermediate stage in preparing plants for the summer garden. They sow vegetable and flower seeds indoors, then transfer the plants to the greenhouse. Most plants destined for the garden grow more compactly and with greater energy in a spring greenhouse—with its bright, sunny days and cool nights—than they would indoors. What's more, they are already hardened off for the summer garden. When summer arrives, the greenhouse covering can be rolled up or, depending on the model, removed entirely. Some models are designed to be dismantled. In the fall, the covering can be restored and tender plants placed under the protective cover.

Many gardeners like to plant heat-loving vegetables, such as tomatoes, cucumbers, peppers, and melons, directly in raised beds under a tunnel-type greenhouse. They either raise or remove the covering during hot weather so that the plants can take advantage of rain and natural breezes, and they restore the covering when the weather cools so that the crops will continue to mature well into the fall.

When you remove the film plastic, be sure to fold it carefully and store it according to the manufacturer's instructions.

Protecting Plants in Winter
Another popular use of seasonal greenhouses is winter protection for plants of doubtful hardiness. Usually, the temperature under the film plastic is several degrees warmer than the outside air. The greenhouse also reduces the drying effects of wind and moderates temperature extremes.

A small electric or gas heater used during the coldest weather will not only protect plants, it will also melt snow from the greenhouse and keep the structure from collapsing—one of the prime dangers of an unheated greenhouse in winter. Once plants are dormant and no longer photosynthesizing, they can be covered with straw or landscape fabric for even greater protection from the cold.

In warmer regions, even where light frosts are a common occurrence, a tunnel-type greenhouse with only a basic heating system is often sufficient to keep tropical plants alive during the winter.

ASSEMBLING THE KIT

After deciding on a greenhouse kit and placing your order, it's time to get ready for the installation. This includes clearing and leveling the site; planning for water, electricity, and heat; and constructing the foundation. Only after you have prepared the groundwork are you ready to install the greenhouse itself.

Planning Utility Services
Greenhouses intended for temporary, seasonal use only can usually make do with electricity from an outdoor extension cord and water from a garden hose. For any other type of greenhouse, you will want to seriously consider permanent, underground wiring and plumbing. Avoid possible problems by planning these connections before the foundation is completed. For more information, see Water and Electrical Hookups on page 27.

If you plan to heat a seasonal structure, you will find that an electric heater is satisfactory. If you prefer a gas or oil heater for a tunnel-type greenhouse, plan on extra ventilation. In more permanent types of greenhouses, adequate ventilation is usually built in. Talk to the supplier about heating systems suited to your climate and to the unit you are buying.

Building the Foundation
The fact that a greenhouse is assembled from a kit rather than built from a plan in no way lessens the need for a proper foundation. An adequate foundation is the basis for a long-lasting, trouble-free greenhouse. The manufacturer's recommendation for a suitable, basic foundation is included with the kit. It is important to follow this minimum requirement, although you can build a more elaborate foundation, if you want to. Certainly, hobbyists in areas where the ground freezes should construct a foundation extending below the frost line. Refer to pages 20 to 26 for step-by-step directions for building a traditional concrete foundation.

Unless you have considerable building experience, think seriously about hiring a professional to install the foundation. Glass or rigid plastic panels will fit properly only if the foundation is perfectly square and plumb. Even a film-covered greenhouse sitting on a poor foundation will be subject to stress that can shorten its life.

A small, simple, lightweight greenhouse like this one can usually be installed by two people in as little as a few hours.

Greenhouses intended for seasonal use require no foundation or else a very light one. They are usually staked to the ground or attached to a simple 2 by 4 frame. Since structures sitting on a light foundation are vulnerable to wind damage, they should be securely anchored. Most kits include stakes for this purpose. Since the greenhouse can be installed on any well-drained, level surface, such as a patio or flat roof, you may need to devise a way to secure the structure without damaging the surface. One method is to fasten the greenhouse to a frame of rot-resistant, heavy timbers. Another method is to run rope over the greenhouse roof and peg the ends of the rope on either side of the paved surface or tie them to nearby objects.

Installing the Greenhouse

Be sure to order your greenhouse kit well ahead of the desired installation date. Although greenhouse companies are careful to ship kits on time, mistakes can occur. Having to delay the installation at the last minute can be costly, especially if you've hired a contractor.

The first step, although not every manufacturer suggests it, is to open the kit and check every part against the master list. All parts are carefully numbered to make this task easier. If anything is missing, contact the supplier immediately. Obviously, it is easier to get missing parts on time if you check the parts list a full week before the installation date. Never spread small parts on a lawn or open ground, as they are too easily lost. It is safer to place them on a tarpaulin or large cloth.

If you are assembling the kit yourself, allow some leeway in the installation date for bad weather. Don't try to put together the greenhouse during windy or rainy weather. Installing glass paneling is extremely risky in windy conditions. Since plastic film must be pulled taut to be effective, it should be applied when the air is calm.

Once the foundation is in place, all the parts are accounted for, and the weather is favorable, you are ready to proceed. Review the plan, or watch the videotape demonstration again. Building a greenhouse from a kit is like working on a jigsaw puzzle; each piece must be placed in its proper position in the right order. Instructions that seem unclear at first become obvious as the installation advances and as you begin to understand the logic.

Never take shortcuts or skip any steps; deviating from the manufacturer's recommendations can lead to serious problems. Most greenhouse kits, especially those with glass or rigid plastic panels, are designed to fit together snugly. If you install parts in the wrong order or disregard the plan, the greenhouse simply will not fit together properly.

Usually, greenhouse manufacturers specify a certain number of days or hours in which their kits can be installed. This ranges from less than one hour for the simplest seasonal greenhouses to about four days, or two weekends, for more elaborate structures. Generally, these figures are based on two people working together. If you and your helper have little construction experience, always assume that the installation will take 50 percent longer.

Tips for Owners of Kit Greenhouses

Your purchased greenhouse will provide many years of satisfaction if you take care of it properly and use it wisely.

• Buy a repair kit from the supplier at the same time that you purchase the greenhouse. Although most greenhouses will remain in good shape long after their guarantees have expired, accidents can happen. Even a temporary repair to a covering that will have to be replaced is better than leaving the interior of the greenhouse exposed to the elements.

• Although most wood members of a greenhouse structure are made of rot-resistant lumber, such as redwood or cedar, you may want to give them extra protection with a waterproofing stain or paint. This can be done before or after assembly.

• Although the more elaborate models usually provide plenty of headroom, some of the less expensive structures don't offer much clearance. Avoid years of stooping by installing the greenhouse on top of foundation walls, or knee walls (see page 25).

• Keep any trees around a film-covered greenhouse properly pruned. Wayward or fallen branches can easily puncture the plastic.

Installation of a large, glass-covered greenhouse is often best left to an expert. You may wish to hire an experienced contractor to help with the project.

Right: Find out as much as you can about available products before purchasing a greenhouse kit. A good starting point is the list of greenhouse sources on the opposite page.

Bottom: A window greenhouse is a relatively inexpensive way to experiment with greenhouse gardening. Order a unit as close as possible to the size of the window opening; if necessary, modify the aperture with 1 by 4 boards.

Window Greenhouses

If you're not ready for a full-scale greenhouse or don't have room for one, a window greenhouse will give you a sense of greenhouse gardening. More than just a collection of plants in a bay window, a real window greenhouse shuts on the inside so that the plants are enclosed in their own greenhouse environment.

Ready-to-install window greenhouses are widely available. Measure the window in which you intend to install the greenhouse and order the closest available size. The unit should be attached to the house framing for stability, so pick a model with a flange nail-ing area just larger than the rough opening. If this is not possible, plan on adding to the framing as needed.

Remove the existing window to accommodate the greenhouse unit. Nail or screw the window greenhouse to the solid wood framing around the rough opening. If the new window is too small, add boards to the inner edges of the opening. You will need help in holding the greenhouse while it is being attached.

Replace the flashing, siding, and trim after the window is installed. Seal all the joints with weatherproofing caulk.

Greenhouse Sources

For a more extensive listing of sources of hobby greenhouses and accessories, send a check for $2.50 to Hobby Greenhouse Association, 8 Glen Terrace, Bedford, MA 01730-2048, 617-275-0377. The Hobby Greenhouse Association is a nonprofit organization of dedicated plant growers interested in providing the latest information to hobby greenhouse owners.

Atlas Greenhouse Systems, Inc.
PO Box 558, Hwy 82 East
Alapaha, GA 31622
800-346-9902 or 912-532-2905
Inexpensive units made of steel tubing frame with 6-mil film plastic; accessories.

Creative Structures, Inc.
281 North West End Blvd.
Quakertown, PA 18951
800-873-3966 or 215-538-2426
Redwood and glass greenhouses and sunrooms; accessories.

Gothic Arch Greenhouses
Box 1564-OR
Mobile, AL 36633-1564
800-628-4974 or 334-432-7529
Arched redwood or cedar greenhouses with acrylic stabilized fiberglass covering; accessories.

Hoop House Greenhouse Kits
Fox Hill Farm
1358 Route 28
South Yarmouth, MA 02664
800-760-5192 or 508-760-5191
Inexpensive units made of steel tubing with 6-mil film plastic; supplies.

Hummert Seed Co.
4500 Earth City Expressway
Earth City MO 63045
314-770-1158
Greenhouse supplies.

Janco Greenhouses
J. A. Nearing Co., Inc.
9390 Davis Avenue
Laurel, MD 20723
301-498-5700 in Maryland
800-323-6933 out of state
Attached and freestanding aluminum and glass greenhouses; solar rooms; accessories.

Northern Light Greenhouses
Gardener's Supply Co.
128 Intervale Road
Burlington VT 05401
802-863-1700 in Vermont
800-688-5510 out of state
Attached and freestanding aluminum and film plastic greenhouses; also hoop-style model; accessories.

Santa Barbara Greenhouses
721 Richmond Ave.
Oxnard CA 93030
800-544-5276 or 805-483-4288
Redwood greenhouses and sunrooms with glass or rigid plastic panels; accessories.

Solar Components Corp.
121 Valley Street
Manchester, NH 03103
603-668-8186;
fax: 603-668-1783
Greenhouses, solariums, and aquaculture containers.

Stuppy Greenhouse Manufacturing, Inc.
Box 12456
North Kansas City, MO 64116
800-733-5025
Greenhouses and supplies for commercial growers; will also sell to hobbyists.

Sturdi-Built Greenhouse Manufacturing, Co.
Department OT
11304 Southwest Boones Ferry Road
Portland, OR 97219
503-244-4100
Attached, freestanding, and custom redwood greenhouses; sunrooms; cold frames; accessories.

Sun Room Design
Depot and First Streets
Youngwood, PA 15697
800-621-1110 or 412-925-1100
Aluminum or wood-clad greenhouses and solariums, accessories.

Sundance Supply
800-776-2534
website: www. sundancesupply.com
Greenhouse components for builders; polycarbonate sheets; glazing system; heating and ventilation equipment.

Sunglo Greenhouses
2626 15th Avenue West
Seattle WA 98119
800-647-0606
Attached and freestanding aluminum and acrylic solar greenhouses; solariums; accessories.

Sunshine Rooms, Inc.
Box 4627
Wichita, KS 67204
800-222-1598
147 models of greenhouses, solariums, and spa enclosures.

Texas Greenhouse Co., Inc.
2524 White Settlement Road
Fort Worth, TX 76107
800-227-5447 or 817-335-5447
Attached and freestanding aluminum and wood greenhouses with choice of glazing; window greenhouses; cold frames; accessories.

Turner Greenhouses
Box 1260
Goldsboro, NC 27530
800-672-4770
Galvanized steel-frame greenhouses with fiberglass or film plastic covering; accessories.

Under Glass Manufacturing Co.
P. O. Box 798
2121 Ulster Avenue
Lake Katrine, NY 12449
914-336-5050
Aluminum-frame greenhouses and solariums; accessories.

Vegetable Factory, Inc.
Department ORT
495 Post Road East
Westport CT 06880
800-221-2550
"Sun-Porch" convertible sun space that converts from insulated winter room to summer screen room.

Many manufacturers of greenhouses and sunrooms designed to be installed by homeowners have internet web sites giving more information about their products. If you have access to a computer with internet capabilities, use the terms greenhouse *and* kit *in the search engine software you use in order to find a list of manufacturers.*

Outfitting the Greenhouse

A well-equipped greenhouse has conveniently arranged benches, its own watering and fertilizing systems, and a plentiful supply of potting mixes.

Working in the greenhouse will be more enjoyable if you plan your space carefully. Lay out the benches so that light is distributed evenly and as much space as possible is devoted to plants. Allow plenty of room to display plants as well as adequate work space for repotting, grooming plants, and starting new plants. Select among the building plans shown beginning on page 61 for benches and storage shelves. Simple to construct, the units are attractive and functional.

So that the plants can get the close attention they need, the well-outfitted greenhouse will have its own watering and fertilizing systems. Hand-watering, sprinklers, drip irrigation, and capillary matting are all watering methods used in greenhouses. Most greenhouse gardeners use water-soluble fertilizers applied by hand, with a siphon proportioner, or through a fertilizer injector attached to a sprinkler or drip system. Choose the methods that appeal to you and that will allow you to give consistent, reliable care to your plants.

Sterile potting mixes contribute to a clean, healthy greenhouse environment. You can purchase a commercial soilless potting mix or make your own from one of the formulas provided on page 69. To make sure you always have potting mix when you need it, store extra batches in heavy-duty plastic bags or clean garbage cans.

This well-arranged greenhouse features a potting bench with separate bins for vermiculite, perlite, and peat moss. Winding the hose neatly around a hose bracket keeps the nozzle off the floor, where it might pick up disease organisms.

Left: A sink is always a welcome addition to a potting area. The sink can be built into the bench, or it can be a freestanding unit. Right: In an aisle plan, there are benches on both sides of the greenhouse and a walkway down the middle.

BENCHES AND POTTING AREA

How greenhouse benches are laid out is very important. A north-south design is preferable, because the benches receive an even distribution of light as the sun moves from east to west. Usually, the layout follows either the aisle or the peninsula plan.

The aisle layout features two rows of benches end to end, generally along each side of the greenhouse to conserve space, with an aisle between. The most common arrangement in hobby greenhouses, the aisle layout often features a small sink and potting area built into one bench.

The peninsula layout has individual benches running in from the walls toward the center of the greenhouse, with very narrow aisles between the benches and a wider aisle down the middle. A sink and potting area often occupy one of the benches. If the greenhouse is big enough, the peninsula plan is probably more satisfactory, because there is room in the center aisle for plants that are brought indoors for the winter.

Whichever system you choose, remember that it costs as much to heat aisle space as it does the space where the plants grow. Therefore, try to plan a layout that allows no more than one quarter to one third of the total floor space for aisles.

Ideally, greenhouse benches should be both practical and good looking. In addition to providing ample display area for plants, the benches should be exposed to the maximum amount of light. The best benches are constructed to allow air to circulate freely through them and among the plants. You can accomplish this by using slats with spaces between them instead of a solid surface for the bench top. For good air flow, there should also be a space between the back of the bench and the greenhouse wall.

Generally, greenhouse bench tops are 32 to 36 inches wide if they can be reached from only one side. In a peninsula layout where they are accessible from both sides, the benches are usually 42 to 48 inches wide. Adjustments can always be made to accommodate your height, reach, and girth.

Make a duplicate of this structure for the back supports. Put the two structures in place in the greenhouse and tie them together with 2 by 4 braces inside the top of each leg and another halfway down.

If you cannot tie the bench to either end of the greenhouse, it is advisable to use one or more diagonal braces underneath. Use 2 by 4s running from the center of a lower brace to the opposite top brace. Cut bird's mouth openings in each for a tight, flush fit to the cross braces.

Once the frame is in place, cover the top with 1 by 4s spaced 1 inch apart. Allow a 6-inch overhang in front. Give the top a finished look by nailing a strip of 1 by 1 half-round molding along the protruding ends. If you want to provide a lip to prevent pots from accidentally being brushed off, use a 1 by 2 for the facing.

For an attractive variation, use lap joints to tie the legs and the top rail together. If you don't have a table saw with a dado blade, make laps by marking each piece, cutting halfway through with a saw and then chiseling out the lap area. The top cross braces can be nailed directly to the inside of each leg where they are hidden, but the lower cross braces should be lap jointed for a truly finished effect.

The sturdiest and longest-lasting benches rest on firm supports, such as bricks or concrete pads, and not just on the ground. Any wood used inside the greenhouse should be naturally rot resistant or else treated with a preservative suitable for use inside greenhouses (see page 65).

Basic Bench

You can make a simple, practical greenhouse bench from 2 by 4 supports and a top of 1 by 4s. Although the top can be as deep as 36 inches for an aisle plan or 48 inches for a peninsula plan, the support structure should be 6 inches narrower than the top. The length of the bench can vary, as long as the legs are spaced evenly, no more than 4 feet apart. The following instructions are for an aisle plan.

Lay the 2 by 4 front legs on a large, flat surface such as a driveway or garage floor. Place them 4 feet apart on center and nail a 2 by 4 rail flush with the top. Use a framing square to make sure the legs are perpendicular to the rail. You should be able to buy one board for the rail for a bench up to 16 feet long.

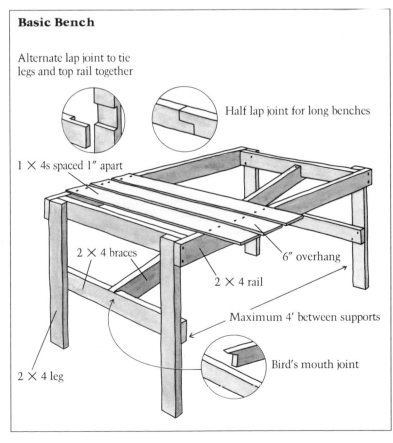

Basic Bench

Alternate lap joint to tie legs and top rail together

Half lap joint for long benches

1 × 4s spaced 1" apart

2 × 4 braces

2 × 4 leg

6" overhang

2 × 4 rail

Maximum 4' between supports

Bird's mouth joint

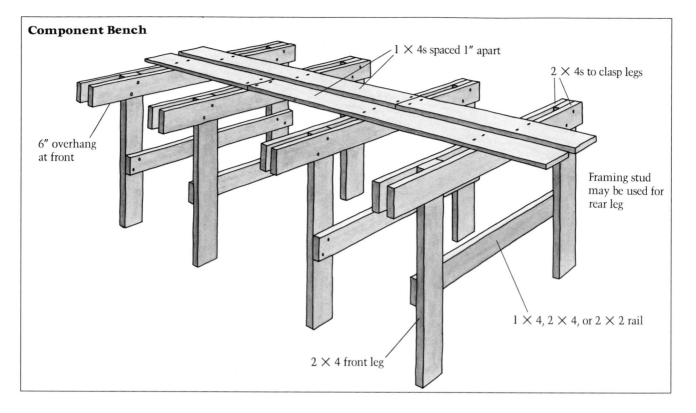

Component Bench

1 × 4s spaced 1″ apart

2 × 4s to clasp legs

6″ overhang at front

Framing stud may be used for rear leg

1 × 4, 2 × 4, or 2 × 2 rail

2 × 4 front leg

Component Bench

This type of bench, which readily adapts itself to any length, can be built in components, or modules. Build the support structure, using 2 by 4s for the front and back legs and clasping each leg at the top between two 2 by 4s extending 6 inches beyond the front leg.

One third the distance up from the bottom of each leg, attach 1 by 4, 2 by 4, or 2 by 2 rails to each pair of legs. These strengthen the bench and also provide lower shelf supports. When the units are all cut and assembled, nail on 1 by 4s horizontally across the bench supports and spaced 1 inch apart.

If the bench is too long for single lengths of the 1 by 4 top, then put the joints on alternate legs so you do not have to rely on one support.

Trough Bench

A trough bench can be the most practical space in the greenhouse. It is suitable for rooting cuttings, growing plants directly in the bench, or holding trays of seedlings until the plants are ready to be moved into the garden.

The usual soil depth in a trough bench is 4 inches. The width of the bench depends on available space; however, more than a 3-foot reach is difficult to manage.

Run two 2 by 4s across upended concrete block legs, using a level to adjust the legs to the same height. Nail bottom boards (1 by 4s or 1 by 6s) to the 2 by 4s, leaving ¼ inch between the boards. Form the sides of the trough by nailing 1 by 6 boards to the bottom boards.

Before filling the bench with potting soil, you can lay newspapers or straw on the bottom to prevent the medium from falling through the cracks.

Other Bench Styles

You can make a pipe-framed bench with 1¼-inch galvanized pipe embedded in concrete piers (half-gallon milk cartons make handy pier forms). Set the complete framework in the forms and brace it; before pouring concrete, check the level. As an alternative, use cinder blocks on end and a framework of either pipe or 2 by 4s.

The top can consist of lath strips or, for a really simple bench, a length of wire mesh or snow fence unrolled onto the rails. Fasten the mesh to the rails and cover the exposed ends of the wire with 1 by 4s.

Wire is widely used as a bench top in greenhouses. Although it provides excellent circulation, it tends to sag. To minimize this, place cross supports every 2 feet. Although useful for flats, cell packs, and large pots, wire mesh may be an unstable surface for small pots, and it may also cause the plants to dry out too fast.

Portable Workbench

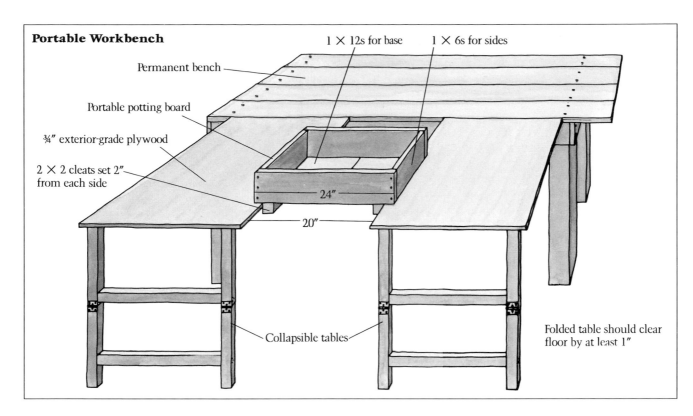

Permanent bench

1 × 12s for base   1 × 6s for sides

Portable potting board

¾″ exterior-grade plywood

2 × 2 cleats set 2″ from each side

24″

20″

Collapsible tables

Folded table should clear floor by at least 1″

Portable Workbench

If you have limited space in your greenhouse but still need to work in it, try a combination of two collapsible tables attached to a permanent bench and a portable potting board that rests on the tables.

Cut the folding tables from ¾-inch exterior-grade plywood that has been treated with a water seal and painted. Each table should be no wider than the height of the potting bench. When folded down, the table should clear the floor by at least 1 inch. You also need to get past the table when it is folded out.

Hinge the plywood top to the top rail of the permanent bench. To make the legs, cut four 2 by 2s of equal length. Put a cross support between two of the leg pieces 2 inches from the bottom, using screws and glue. On the remaining leg pieces, attach a cross support 4 inches from the bottom. Connect the leg sections with hinges, then attach the connected legs to the table with hinges. When the table is not in use, the legs fold up and the top drops down. Magnetic or friction catches can be added to hold the legs up when the table is folded.

Put two of these tables side by side with a 20-inch space between them. The portable potting board that rests on the tables can be 24 inches wide, allowing a 2-inch overlap on each side. Reduce all dimensions if space is tight.

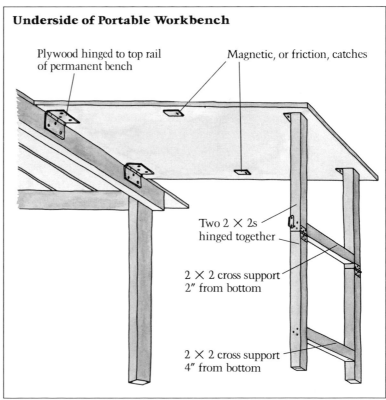

Underside of Portable Workbench

Plywood hinged to top rail of permanent bench

Magnetic, or friction, catches

Two 2 × 2s hinged together

2 × 2 cross support 2″ from bottom

2 × 2 cross support 4″ from bottom

Make the base of the potting board using two 1 by 12s. Tie the base together with 2 by 2 cleats underneath that are set in 2 inches from each side to keep the potting board from slipping when set between the two foldout tables. Make the sides using 1 by 6s.

Left and right:
Hanging pots as well
as wall-mounted and
freestanding shelves
provide extra space
for plants in these
small greenhouses.

Shelves

Once all the benches are filled, most greenhouse owners start looking for more room. In addition to hanging individual potted plants from the greenhouse supports, you can create additional space by building some simple overhead shelves.

To make a rack that holds several pots of the same size, lay out two lengths of 2 by 2 and then nail on 2 by 2 crosspieces spaced just far enough apart to catch the rims of the pots. For a finished appearance, each crosspiece can be lap jointed and painted. Use thin wire to suspend the framework from eyebolts. Each rack should be as long as the overhead supports are spaced, usually 2 or 4 feet on center. If the shelves are 4 feet or longer, run support wires down to their center.

Another useful shelf, especially for those who grow their own bedding plants, consists of 1 by 6s or 1 by 8s in a convenient length suspended from wire loops or supported with shelf brackets.

Potting Area

Some gardeners prefer their potting area outside, in a lath structure. But others, especially those in snowy regions, want their potting area inside the greenhouse where it is conveniently accessible the year around.

The potting area should be located in the northeast corner of the greenhouse where it will block the least amount of sun. It should meet several basic requirements: a flat surface with sides 4 to 6 inches high to keep soil from spilling over; a handy tool storage area; and room under the bench for potting mixes, fertilizers, and other supplies.

Build the bench supports as you would for one of the benches described previously; for the top use either exterior-grade plywood or 1 by 2s butted up against each other. Instead of a solid surface, you can use slats with spaces between them, but then you will need to position a catch basin for soil underneath the bench. If the basin, or tub, is shallow enough, there will still be room for storage shelves below.

A small sink is a convenient, although not essential, addition to the potting area. The sink can be set directly into the bench by resting it on two 2 by 4 braces. The sink top should be flush with the bench top for easy cleanup.

Most plumbing codes require that the sink drain be tied into your house system, but since so little water is normally run through a greenhouse sink, you may be able to pipe it directly onto a nearby plant or tree. In snow country the drain will have to stay below the freezing level, and you may want to run it into a dry well filled with stones. Consult your local building department.

Below-bench storage   You can create a storage area under the potting bench simply by running 1 by 4 slats across the braces. If you have small children, you may want to install cabinet doors on the lower shelves. Good cabinet doors are made just like a gate.

Lay out two 1 by 4s horizontally about 18 inches apart and place 1 by 4 slats vertically on them, leaving a 1-inch space between each slat. Use a framing square as you nail the slats in place with finishing nails. Then turn the door over and recheck it for squareness. Cut a diagonal brace and put it in place, with one end against the lower hinge. After the cabinet door is hung on hinges, use magnetic catches or a bolt to fasten it in front.

Overhead storage If the shape of your greenhouse permits, you can use 1 by 12s to build overhead shelving for the potting area. A handy unit is 3 feet wide and as long as the available space. It is constructed like a box with simple butt joints that are nailed and glued. Put several shelves 6, 12, and 18 inches apart to handle your different storage needs. When the shelves are in, back the boxes with a piece of hardboard or other rigid material. If you want the back open for more light, use galvanized angle braces inside all corners.

If there is an outside wall on which to mount these boxes, you won't need a backing or braces. Cut a 2 by 4 to fit across the inside of the box at the top. Fasten that 2 by 4 to the wall with lag screws sunk into the studs, and then hang the box from it. Put another 2 by 4 support under the lowest shelf to keep the box from swaying. Attach the box to the wall support with one screw at the top and another at the bottom.

If you want cabinet doors, cut them to fit from ½-inch plywood and attach them with butt hinges.

Tool rack A tool rack is handy above the potting area and between two overhead storage shelves. Build one that is ideal for holding the small trowels, shears, scissors, spoons, and brushes that go with potting.

You can make a simple tool rack by cutting a piece of pegboard to fit the area; frame all the edges on the back with 1 by 2 furring strips, including one down the center. This is to keep the pegboard away from the wall so you can insert the metal tool hangers. Put vertical 2 by 2s on each side and then glue and nail a 1 by 2 across the bottom to make a narrow shelf. Come up 6 inches and place a 1 by 2 across the front as the retainer for tools.

Materials Inside the Greenhouse

Except for naturally rot-resistant wood, such as redwood, cedar, and cypress, all wood inside the greenhouse should be treated with a preservative. You can coat untreated lumber with a wood preservative or buy lumber that has already been treated under pressure.

Oil-borne preservatives, such as creosote and pentachlorophenol, should not be used in a greenhouse because they release fumes harmful to plants. Do not coat wood with these products, and make sure that any pressure-treated lumber you buy does not contain these materials.

The most common wood preservatives in greenhouses are copper naphthenate and zinc naphthenate. Copper naphthenate is a dark green solution that turns wood a pale green; covering the treated wood with paint is not recommended. Zinc naphthenate is a clear solution that does not discolor wood; you can apply paint on treated wood. Carefully follow the label directions when using these products.

It is preferable to apply these preservatives outdoors and let the lumber dry thoroughly before moving it into the greenhouse. If you must paint indoors, clear out the plants and vent the greenhouse.

Any metal used in the greenhouse—angle irons, nails, screws, and other hardware—should be galvanized to protect it from corrosion caused by moisture. For greater durability, use hinges made of stainless steel or other high-quality noncorrosive materials.

All interior wood should be naturally rot resistant or treated with a preservative suitable for use inside a greenhouse. Screws, hinges, and other hardware will last longer if they are made from a noncorrosive material.

A fan nozzle slows the flow of water from the garden hose.

WATERING AND FERTILIZING SYSTEMS

Because their roots are restricted in containers, plants in a greenhouse need more frequent watering and feeding than the same plants in a garden bed. Yet excess water and nutrients can spell disaster for greenhouse plants. Select the irrigation and fertilizing methods that fit your budget and that make it easy for you to tend your plants properly.

Watering

The most common watering systems for a greenhouse are hand-watering with a garden hose or watering can, overhead sprinklers and misters, drip irrigation, and capillary matting. Whichever system you use, it is best to group plants according to moisture need and to water in the morning so that foliage dries by evening.

Hand-watering   This is the way most hobby greenhouses are irrigated. Watering a large number of plants with a garden hose or watering can is time consuming. However, it gives you the chance to judge whether a particular plant needs water. Unlike sprinklers and other systems that water all plants on the system, hand-watering allows you to skip plants that have sufficient moisture.

Use nozzles—a water breaker on a hose and a rose attachment on a watering can—to slow the flow of water and direct it into gentle streams. These nozzles should never be left on the floor, where they can pick up bacteria and other disease organisms.

Overhead sprinklers and misters   In a hobby greenhouse, low-volume sprinklers are more appropriate than the conventional sprinklers used to water large commercial greenhouses. Low-volume systems run on lower pressure and throw water a shorter distance. A common arrangement consists of a series of overlapping half-circle sprays; 180-degree nozzles are inserted in PVC pipe or polyethylene tubing running along both sides of the greenhouse bench. Wiring the valve to a timer automates the system.

The main purpose of misters, which emit a fine spray, is to maintain humidity in the greenhouse. Also used to irrigate a propagation bench (see page 104), misters are not intended as a general watering system.

Greenhouse Sanitation

Before starting on your first greenhouse growing project, it is important to sterilize the interior of the greenhouse. Probably the quickest, easiest, most economical, and safest way is to wash everything down with a broom and a bucket of water to which a pint of liquid household bleach has been added. Scrub all the crevices and crannies of benches, side walls, and floors.

Take measures to maintain a clean, healthy environment. Don't leave hose nozzles or tools lying on the floor. Regularly clean the benches as well as used pots and flats with a bleach solution. When bringing new plants into the greenhouse, quarantine them in a separate area (even a screen-covered box) for a few days to make sure they aren't carrying pests that may be transmitted to other plants. Since prevention is simpler than eradication, inspect plants in the greenhouse on a regular basis. Nip any problems right away; don't wait for them to get out of hand.

Drip irrigation A drip system is one in which water is applied slowly through emitters or through perforations in a pipe or hose.

Perforated tubing is useful for watering a trough bench. To water individually potted plants, run ½-inch polyethylene drip tubing down the middle of the bench and branch off at intervals with short lengths of microtubing with emitters at the ends. Small plastic stakes can be used to hold the emitters in place. Some greenhouse owners use perforated lead weights that dispense water as well as hold the tubing in the pot. Connect the main tubing to a faucet and add a timer to automate the system.

Capillary matting This type of system waters the plants from below. Potted plants are placed on a wetted mat from which they draw moisture by capillary action. The pots must have drainage holes so that water can enter.

To set up the system, first cover an entire bench with plastic sheeting to protect it. Over it lay a capillary mat, available from greenhouse suppliers; you can substitute an absorbent material, such as old outdoor carpet or a flannel blanket. Make sure the mat does not extend over the edges of the bench. Wet the mat and set potted plants on it.

Instead of manually watering the capillary mat, you can add a drip hose controlled by a timer to wet the mat at regular intervals.

Fertilizing

Greenhouse plants generally grow best when given small but frequent dosages of fertilizer. The trend today is to use water-soluble fertilizers, because you can water and feed at the same time. Dry granular feeds can be used, but they are more time consuming to apply and must be watered in well to dissolve the fertilizer; the plants must also be leached more often to get rid of accumulated salts.

You can hand-feed by mixing a dilute fertilizer solution and applying it with a watering can. A safe concentration consists of one fifth of the amount called for on the label for a monthly application. If the label calls for 1 tablespoon to 1 gallon of water, make the dilution 1 tablespoon to 5 gallons of water.

A more sophisticated method utilizes a siphon proportioner to dispense the fertilizer automatically as you water. Because the proportioner adds 1 part fertilizer to 16 parts

water, you must make the solution 16 times stronger than the package directs you to. If the label calls for 1 tablespoon to 1 gallon water, use 16 times that amount—16 tablespoons, or 1 cup, in 1 gallon water.

The siphoning tube goes into the bucket of fertilizer solution. Attach one end of the siphoner to the faucet, and connect the other end to the hose. As you water the plants, fertilizer is siphoned from the bucket and mixed in with the water.

Top: Individual drip emitters supply slow, uniform irrigation to greenhouse plants. The emitters are connected to microtubing, which in turn is attached to ½-inch polyethylene tubing leading to the water supply and a timer.
Left: Capillary matting is a simple, effective way of watering plants from below. Water is drawn up into the potted plant by capillary action.

Top: This potting area features a trough bench filled with a sterile potting mix and an extensive bench top for holding seeded trays and flats. Bottom: Perlite is often used as a rooting medium. It anchors cuttings, drains quickly, and holds air and water well.

Fertilizer injectors are available for drip and sprinkler systems. Fill the cartridge or canister with water-soluble fertilizer; during irrigation, it is diluted at the correct rate and injected into the system. If the injector doesn't have a built-in antisiphon device to keep fertilizer from accidentally getting into the potable water system, attach a separate backflow preventer.

Time-release fertilizers are another popular way to feed greenhouse plants. Nutrients become available in small amounts as the plant is watered. These fertilizers come in many forms, such as pellets and spikes. Some can be mixed with the soil before planting; others can be hammered into or buried in the soil.

POTTING MIXES

Any soil used in the greenhouse should be porous, and it should drain well while retaining moisture for plants to draw on. The soil must be free of diseases and weeds as well. Since greenhouse plants may remain in the same pot for months or years, the soil should also be relatively stable—that is, it shouldn't expand or shrink a great deal.

Soilless mixes are commonly used in greenhouses. Not only do most have the characteristics described above, but they are also sterile. This is highly desirable in a clean, controlled environment like a greenhouse. Soilless mixes are low in nutrients, however, and require regular fertilizer.

Some gardeners who have a compost pile and a friable garden soil that is relatively free of insects and diseases like to mix these materials with a soilless potting mix to stretch their supply of greenhouse soil.

A soilless potting mix consists of organic materials—such as peat moss, redwood sawdust, and fir bark—as well as minerals. Among the most common minerals in potting soils are vermiculite, perlite, and fine sand. Used for aeration, vermiculite and perlite are mined materials that expand to 20 times their original volume when subjected to high temperatures. You can also use either of these materials for starting seeds or rooting cuttings.

A relatively new addition to some potting mixes, polystyrene beads are a product of the plastics industry. The material is usually manufactured from recycled fast-food containers. The beads, which do not break down, have a tendency to float. Many commercial growers find that mixing them with sand and peat moss helps to bind them into the mix.

Rock wool is another relatively new material used as an ingredient in soilless potting mixes. Used extensively in Europe, rock wool is a natural material made by blowing steam through molten rock. Inert and sterile, it retains oxygen and water. Rock wool can be used alone, mixed with peat moss, or incorporated into a commercial soilless mix.

Rock wool is available in growing blocks for starting seeds or cuttings. A mixture of rock wool and peat moss is available in polyethylene bags that lay flat on a bench or the floor; make slits in the bag and insert the seeds or cuttings directly into the medium.

Homemade Mixes

When you need only a few cubic feet of a potting mix, your best bet is to buy a commercial product. For larger quantities, you may choose to make your own mix.

Blend large amounts of potting mix on a smooth surface such as a concrete driveway or a patio. Layer the ingredients, making a flat-topped mound a foot or so high. With a shovel keep turning the pile until it looks homogeneous. Store the mix in heavy-duty plastic bags or clean garbage cans.

Each of the following formulas makes about 1 cubic yard. For smaller amounts of potting soil, substitute half-gallons for cubic feet and ounces for pounds.

Lightweight mix   This mix is suitable for both seedlings and more mature potted plants.
9 cubic feet peat moss
9 cubic feet vermiculite
9 cubic feet perlite
5 pounds 5-10-10 fertilizer
5 pounds ground limestone

Medium-weight mix   This is a slightly heavier version of the potting mix listed above. It is suitable for seedlings as well as for older potted plants.
7 cubic feet fine sand
14 cubic feet peat moss
7 cubic feet perlite
5 pounds 5-10-10 fertilizer
8 pounds ground limestone

Foliage houseplant mix   Use this mix for indoor foliage plants in the greenhouse as well as in the home.
14 cubic feet peat moss
7 cubic feet vermiculite
7 cubic feet perlite
5 pounds 5-10-10 fertilizer
1 pound iron sulfate
8 pounds ground limestone

Shrub and tree mix   This combination is suitable for woody plants that will be transplanted into the garden as well as those that will be kept indefinitely in pots in the greenhouse.
9 cubic feet fine sand
18 cubic feet ground bark or
   nitrogen-stabilized sawdust

For a coarser mix combine the following.
9 cubic feet fine sand
9 cubic feet peat moss
9 cubic feet ground bark
Add the following to either of the above formulas.
5 pounds 5-10-10 fertilizer
1 pound iron sulfate
7 pounds ground limestone

Top: Adequately watered and fertilized plants have a better chance of succeeding in a greenhouse. Bottom: Plastic garbage containers under the potting bench are a convenient place to store soil mix.

Managing the Greenhouse

By carefully controlling the temperature, humidity, and light inside the greenhouse, you are creating an artificial environment in which plants not only survive but flourish.

Although the exterior of a greenhouse is exposed to wide extremes in temperature, the interior climate must be carefully regulated so that plants don't freeze in winter or overheat in summer. In the winter it's difficult to know just how much heat is required. Unless you seal and insulate the greenhouse, heat will flow out at an alarming—and costly—rate. In the summer, sunlight can raise the indoor temperature to suffocating levels unless the greenhouse is properly ventilated and cooled. If vents and fans aren't enough, consider an evaporative cooler and greenhouse shading.

The humidity level in a greenhouse must be within tolerable limits. Many greenhouse owners water the floor daily or install a mist system to maintain humidity. Excess humidity can be a greater problem than lack of moisture in the air. Guard against a buildup of condensation by insulating the greenhouse and circulating the warm air.

Managing light—exposing plants to the light levels they need for healthy growth—is also critical. Knowing where a plant originated will give you a clue about its light requirement. A greenhouse provides the opportunity for experimentation: Learn how to manipulate light to force plants into bloom anytime of the year.

Proper management of the greenhouse environment is essential for healthy plant growth. Shading on the plastic wall panels cuts down on sunlight and heat inside the greenhouse during the hottest part of the year.

A well-insulated greenhouse requires less supplemental heat during cold weather.

HEATING THE GREENHOUSE

The basic considerations in heating a greenhouse are to provide adequate heat and to distribute it evenly—at a reasonable cost. The heating system should be automated so that it is activated only when the temperature dips below a certain level. It should be designed to use the least costly fuel available, and to minimize problems the system should be as simple and straightforward as possible.

With these considerations in mind, use as many solar heating techniques as you can to conserve energy and lessen the need for supplemental heat. Ways of capturing and storing solar heat are discussed in the solar greenhouse section beginning on page 86.

Whatever type of heater you choose—oil, electric, gas, or gas-fired infrared waves—you must keep the air moving to prevent the heat from collecting at the top of the greenhouse.

You will need two fans, one connected to the heating unit and a moderate-sized, two-speed fan near the top of the roof to circulate the air downward. The upper fan, which does not need a thermostat, should be kept running continuously, day and night.

The upper fan is also the cheapest and simplest way to control diseases in a greenhouse. All leaf diseases caused by bacteria or fungi start in a droplet or film of water lying on the plant surface. Even viruses are spread more quickly when foliage is wet. Keeping leaves dry is the best way to reduce the incidence of such diseases as gray mold, downy mildew, leaf spot, and anthracnose.

Any thermostat for heating or cooling equipment should be located away from direct sunlight. It can be mounted on a wall under a shelf or protected in a small box.

It is a good idea to safeguard against power failure or drastically changing temperatures. You can install a battery-operated alarm connected to your house to signal any radical drop in temperature. Another safeguard against temperature change is a small electric space heater with a built-in thermostat that turns on if the temperature falls below a certain point.

Before you install a heating system, check for cracks around vents, doors, and glazing panes. These small leaks allow large amounts of heat to escape. Counteract this heat loss with a lining of 4-mil polyethylene film. For the best results use two layers, either inflating them (see page 38) or keeping a ¾- to 4-inch space between the layers. This air pocket between the two layers helps insulate the greenhouse.

If combustion air for the heating system comes from inside the greenhouse, you must leave one or two small cracks; otherwise, the flame will go out. Insufficient outside air can cause incomplete combustion, resulting in epinasty (twisting and curling of leaves) when gas-fired heaters are used. To let in outside air, leave a small space equal to about 1 square inch of opening for each 2,000 BTUs (British thermal units).

Estimating Your Heating Needs

The local utility company can help estimate your heating needs based on the size, construction, and glazing of the greenhouse. You can make your own rough estimate with the following calculations.

First, determine the total surface area (SA) by multiplying the length times the height of each wall and of the roof. Don't count the floor. Add these numbers to determine the total area in square feet.

Left: This foliage is kept dry because of a roof fan overhead. Many diseases begin in droplets of water on the leaf surface. Right: A thermometer and a relative humidity gauge are indispensable for monitoring the temperature and humidity in a greenhouse.

Second, calculate the degree rise (DR). This is the difference between the coldest outdoor temperature recorded in the last several years and the temperature you want to maintain in the greenhouse. Find out the low temperature from the weather bureau. If you want to maintain a greenhouse temperature of 55° F (13° C) and the lowest expected temperature is 15° F (-9° C), then the degree rise is 40° F (4° C).

Next, consider the insulating factors (IF) for the type of glazing on your greenhouse.

Glazing	Calm	Windy
Glass	1.5	1.8
Fiberglass or polyethylene	1.2	1.4
Double layer (glass/plastic)	0.8	1.0

Now, multiply the above figures: $SA \times DR \times IF$. The result is the heat loss per hour in BTUs. The heater output for your greenhouse should be equal to the heat loss calculated with this formula.

Most heaters are labeled with their rated BTU output. In order to convert BTUs to kilowatts for electric heaters labeled in kilowatts, divide the answer to the formula by 3,413.

Saving Energy

Here are some simple steps you can take to conserve energy in the greenhouse.
• Line the greenhouse with a double layer of film plastic. To create an insulating air pocket, either inflate the layers (see page 38) or leave a ¾- to 4-inch space between them. Two layers of film plastic transmit only 15 percent less sunlight than a single layer but reduce heat loss by about 42 percent.
• Keep the greenhouse cool at night. Germinating seeds need constant warmth, but heat can be confined to a small propagator (see instructions for building a seed-starting chamber on page 99). As soon as seeds have germinated and show green, they can tolerate a temperature of 50° F (10° C).
• Grow plants that have relatively low temperature requirements or short production periods. Cineraria, calceolaria, primrose, and cyclamen are among the plants that respond best to cool conditions.

• Plant low-growing shrubs around the foundation of your greenhouse. They will prevent heat loss by deflecting the wind and trapping the snow.
• Use a windbreak to reduce heat loss from a glass-covered greenhouse. In a 15-mile-per-hour wind the greenhouse loses heat twice as fast as it does when the air is still. Either plant a living windbreak of low-branching evergreens or use an artificial windbreak, such as a snow fence made with 1-inch slats or woven polypropylene netting. Ideally, a windbreak should be positioned 40 to 60 feet to the windward side of the greenhouse and 25 feet beyond the ends of the greenhouse.

The effect of a windbreak in reducing heat loss from a greenhouse covered with film plastic or rigid plastic is not as great as with a glass-covered one, because the plastic materials have fewer cracks and joints.

COOLING THE GREENHOUSE

In northern climates you may not have a cooling problem: Opening the vents in the wall and roof may be enough. This is probably true if summer temperatures rarely exceed 80° F (27° C). The vents can be opened manually, or thermal pistons can be installed for automatic opening and closing. The pistons expand with heat to open the vents and then contract when the temperature drops. They have controls that can be set to your needs.

In hotter regions, cooling the greenhouse in the summer may be a bigger problem than heating it in winter. In these areas, plan on supplementing vents with other cooling methods. In addition to the two-speed, continuously running fan in the peak of the greenhouse (see Heating the Greenhouse, page 72), hook up other fans that will turn on when the temperature rises beyond a certain point. You may also need to shade the greenhouse and install an evaporative cooler.

Shading the Greenhouse

There are many ways to shade a greenhouse. Opaque plastic, bamboo, or aluminum screens can be mounted on the roof and rolled down when protection is needed. These are also useful for protecting glass roofs in areas with heavy hailstorms. Green vinyl comes in rolls

Top: There are many manual methods for opening roof vents. In this greenhouse, turning a wheel opens the vent. Right: A series of roof vents helps cool this glass greenhouse.

that can be cut to fit inside your windows; simply wet the windows and apply the plastic with a squeegee.

Whitewash, formerly a common shading for greenhouses, is corrosive and no longer recommended. Today there are a variety of improved, water-soluble commercial shade compounds in both powder and liquid forms. The liquid form is less troublesome and does not ruin spray equipment. Special sticker or binder liquids can be added to make the material adhere longer. You can even make your own shade compound from equal parts of powdered milk and flour. An excellent temporary shade, it washes off easily.

In tests of commercial shade compounds at Colorado State University, it was found that white shading reflected about 83 percent solar radiation; green reflected 43 percent; and blue or purple, 25 percent.

When applying a shade compound, start with a very light application and add more if needed. Apply the shading during typical weather conditions since that is the best time to judge the effect of the application. If you live in an area where clear skies are usual, apply the shading at noon on a sunny day. If your weather is typically cloudy, paint on the shading at noon on an overcast day.

Don't overshade: It is better to have too much light in a greenhouse than not enough. Also, a shading compound that is applied too heavily may be difficult to remove. You may need a scrub brush, although plastic glazings such as polycarbonate, acrylic, and polyvinyl are easily scratched and may suffer a permanent reduction in light transmission. Most of the plastic glazings available today have built-in shading characteristics. The presence of condensates in the covering reduces light transmission.

Creating shade in other ways Plants can be used to create natural shade in the greenhouse. For example, a heat- and sun-loving vine like bougainvillea trained on a support near the greenhouse wall will cast dappled shade. This shady area is ideal for camellias, rhododendrons, and other plants that must be shielded from the sun.

You can also train annual vines up a trellis propped against the south-facing exterior greenhouse wall. Remove the vines and trellis in winter so that the sun's rays aren't blocked when they are most needed.

Using double-decked benches—one bench perched 2½ to 3 feet above another—is another good way to create a shady microclimate. The top bench will shade the lower bench for most of the day. Place sun-loving plants on the top bench and those requiring shadier conditions on the lower bench. Be sure to water plants on the top bench twice as often as those in the shade.

Left: Shade-loving plants grow better in the dim environment beneath a greenhouse bench. Right: A shade cloth is placed on the curved walls of this greenhouse during hot, sunny weather.

Installing an Evaporative Cooler

Shading helps, but in many regions you will need some artificial cooling for an effective greenhouse. One of the best and most economical devices is the evaporative cooler, often called a swamp cooler or pad-and-fan cooler. You can buy one, or you can make your own for a fraction of the price. The basic principle is simple: A fan draws outside air through a constantly wet pad; this cools the inside air and at the same time increases the humidity.

A few simple calculations are required for setting up an evaporative cooler. Fans are rated in cubic feet per minute (cfm)—this refers to the number of cubic feet of air they can move every minute. To find the cubic feet of space in your greenhouse, multiply the length and the width of the greenhouse by the average height of the roof. An 8- by 12-foot greenhouse has 96 square feet of floor space. At an average roof height of 10 feet, the total space is 960 cubic feet.

In commercial greenhouses the air is usually exchanged every minute. Since a home greenhouse has a smaller volume that heats up much faster, plan on exchanging the air twice a minute. If your greenhouse has a volume of 960 cubic feet, you will want a fan that can move twice that amount of air every minute, or about 2,000 cfm.

The exhaust fan should be mounted high up, usually over the door, to pull out the hottest air. The cooling pad should be located at the opposite end of the greenhouse and ideally at the same level as the plants.

Previously, most pads were made of aspen shavings, excelsior, or plastic. Now on the market are cellulose pads impregnated with insoluble antirot salts. Another modern cooling pad system consists of a bonded plastic fiber pad coated with an absorbent cellular foam. Unaffected by continual exposure to moisture, disinfectants, chlorine, or water acidity, these new pads are so efficient that you do not even see water trickling down the side. All of the new evaporative cooling pads fit existing systems; they are easy to install and clean.

The size of the pad is important. It is determined by dividing the required air flow by 150. Thus, an 8- by 12-foot greenhouse needing an air exchange of 2,000 cfm requires about 13 square feet of pad (2,000 ÷ 150 = 13.3). The

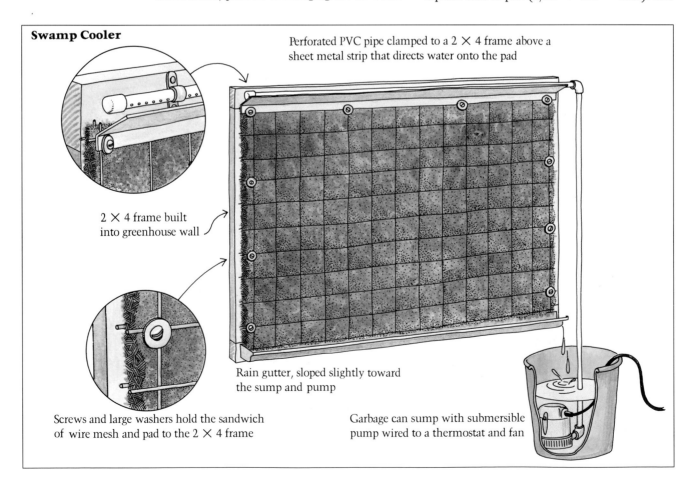

Swamp Cooler

Perforated PVC pipe clamped to a 2 × 4 frame above a sheet metal strip that directs water onto the pad

2 × 4 frame built into greenhouse wall

Rain gutter, sloped slightly toward the sump and pump

Screws and large washers hold the sandwich of wire mesh and pad to the 2 × 4 frame

Garbage can sump with submersible pump wired to a thermostat and fan

Left: Regularly watering the gravel floor is an easy, effective way to maintain humidity in the greenhouse.
Right: The lobster claw (Heliconia species), a tropical flowering plant, requires high humidity. It should be grouped with other moisture-loving plants and misted regularly.

most effective pad is one that extends across the entire wall.

The pad should be cut to size and then clamped between wire mesh to prevent it from sagging. Cut the greenhouse wall opening to size and frame it with 2 by 4 redwood or other rot-resistant lumber. On the lower support, mount a section of rain gutter angled slightly for water runoff. Fasten the screen and pad in place between the frame with screws and washers for easy removal.

At the lower end of the rain gutter, stand a plastic garbage can with a circulating pump that supplies about ⅓ gallon per minute per lineal foot of pad, regardless of the pad's height. The sump, or plastic container, should have a capacity of 1¼ gallons for each lineal foot of pad in order to hold the water that drains back when the system stops.

The water is distributed by a PVC pipe clamped to the 2 by 4 just above the pad. Drill a close series of ⅛-inch holes in the pipe and, for better distribution of the water, put a small strip of sheet metal under the pipe to spread the water onto the pad.

The pump and fan are generally hooked to the same thermostat so they start at the same time. A slightly more sophisticated hookup operates in two stages: The fan starts when the temperature hits 70° F (21° C), and the water starts moving when the temperature reaches 80° F (27° C). Since the fan draws air through any crack, make sure the greenhouse is tightly sealed so that air comes through the pad only.

You must remove the cooling pad when the hot weather ends and replace that section of the greenhouse wall. Seal it well so that it is not a conduit for heat loss during the winter.

CONTROLLING HUMIDITY

When the humidity in the greenhouse is too low, plant growth suffers. High humidity makes many plants grow better, but when it is over 90 percent for any length of time, the risk of leaf mold, stem rot, and other problems increases.

Low humidity is generally corrected by misting or watering the floor two or three times a day to build up water content in the air. Only in extremely arid areas is a humidifier needed in a greenhouse, particularly if an evaporative cooler is used.

Too much humidity is the usual problem, especially during cold weather. The air in the greenhouse flows along the cold windows and cools so rapidly it can no longer hold its moisture. It then condenses onto the glazing. The roof and walls may be so loaded with condensation that it seems to be raining inside. If the leaves have a chance to dry out before nightfall, the risk to the plants is not too severe. When the leaves are damp during the night, however, serious problems can arise.

Insulating the greenhouse will reduce the problem of excess humidity. One solution is to line the inside of the greenhouse with a double layer of film plastic, leaving an air space between the layers. Another solution is to cover the outside of the glazing at night to prevent a collision of warm and cold air. A fan to keep the warm air circulating also helps reduce condensation.

Installing a Mist System

If you live in an arid region where you must fight high temperatures and low humidity much of the year, a mist system is a good way to maintain moisture in the greenhouse. And whether or not your greenhouse is located in a dry climate, a mist system is extremely useful for propagating plants.

If you are misting only a small section of the greenhouse, you can hang clear plastic around the misters to keep other areas dry.

If you have an automated sprinkler or drip system in your greenhouse, you can probably hook the mist system to the same controller. A mist system can also be controlled independently; it can be set up with two timers, one to turn the system on during the day and off at night, and another to run the spray nozzles every few minutes when the system is on. Set the timing sequence yourself, based on what your plants need. The spray nozzles should be activated only when the leaves are dry and they should run only long enough to thoroughly wet all the foliage. (This can be as many as 20 times an hour in very hot, dry climates.)

The problem with timer-operated controls is that they don't take into consideration overcast conditions, when there is less evaporation from the leaves. This produces a tendency to supply too much moisture. Newer systems use a balance rod with a piece of screen on one end and the other end hooked to an on-off switch. When water builds up on the screen, as it would on a leaf, the rod dips and shuts off all the misters; when the water has evaporated, the rod rises and switches the misters back on.

Creating Humid Microclimates

Some plants, particularly many tropical species, thrive in a very humid environment. Most plants do well when the relative humidity is between 50 and 70 percent, but some tropical plants fare best when the level is around 80 percent. Instead of increasing humidity generally in the greenhouse, you can create humid microclimates for these plants.

An easy way to accomplish this is to place the moisture-loving plants on a shallow tray filled with pebbles and water. The water should come up to just below the top of the pebbles so that the roots are not sitting in water. The constant evaporation of the water raises the humidity level around the plants. Be sure to renew the water in the tray regularly.

A mist spray keeps humidity high in the greenhouse. An automated system using a moisture sensor turns the misters on only when they are needed.

UNDERSTANDING LIGHT

Light is one of the most important requirements for healthy plant growth. Without light there would be no photosynthesis—the process by which all green plants manufacture food from water and carbon dioxide. All plants need light, but the amount of light required varies from species to species. Knowing where a plant originated will give you a clue about its light requirement. For example, a plant from a forest floor needs less light than a desert plant. In general, flowering plants require twice as much light as foliage plants.

Technically, light is the visible portion of the electromagnetic wavelength spectrum. It is a blend of red, orange, yellow, green, blue, and violet rays. Plants absorb primarily the blue and red rays; blue rays promote foliage growth and red rays affect several growth processes including flowering. Plants reflect green and yellow rays.

The most important qualities of light for plants are intensity and duration. Generally a plant surviving at a low light intensity only maintains itself; more light enables it to grow better. A plant slowly weakens and eventually dies when the light intensity dips below the minimum that plant can tolerate. A plant deprived of light may appear healthy for some months, but it is living on stored energy and is slowly declining.

Botanists use the word *etiolated* to describe plants grown in very low light or darkness. Etiolated plants are typically spindly; they grow taller because they are reaching for light. Their color is pale and their leaves poorly developed. Seedlings given inadequate light grow tall but then fall over from their own weight.

Plants exposed to light intensities that are too high show variable symptoms. Leaves may wilt during the hottest part of the day, or they may curl downward and develop brown, burned spots. The foliage may turn yellow or burn outright. For instance, orchids exposed to excessive light intensity develop blackened areas on the leaves.

Plants should never be subjected to sudden changes in light. A plant adapted to shade can suffer fatal burning when suddenly moved to a sunny spot. If the move is gradual, the plant may be able to tolerate the change. The results can be compared to a person, pale from winter indoors, going to the beach and getting severely burned by spending too many hours in the sun.

In addition to allowing nighttime gardening, artificial lights can be used to lengthen the day and force certain plants into bloom.

The Light Spectrum

Blue and violet rays promote foliage growth. Plants grown under blue light alone are compact with lush, dark green leaves and few flowers. Red light affects flowering. Yellow and green rays have no major effect on plant growth.

White light passing through a prism or raindrops divides into its component colors. The result is a rainbow.

Measuring Light

Light is measured in footcandles or lumens, depending on whether you are considering the object that is lighted or the source of the light. Natural sunlight and artificial light falling on a plant are measured in footcandles; the light emitted by such sources as the sun itself and electric lamps is rated in lumens.

One footcandle (f.c.) is the amount of visible light falling on 1 square foot of surface located 1 foot away from 1 standard candle. For example, a clear summer day may measure 10,000 f.c. and an overcast winter day as little as 500 f.c. The light of the full moon registers less than 1 f.c. To read comfortably, you need about 20 f.c. Knowing the number of footcandles of light present in various parts of the greenhouse helps you determine where to place plants. Most flowering plants and vegetables need at least 1,000 f.c. (and prefer up to 2,000 f.c.), whereas many foliage plants can get by in as little as 100 f.c. For germinating seeds and rooting cuttings, you generally need between 600 and 2,000 f.c.

The most accurate way to measure the light is with a special light meter that reads directly in footcandles. You can get an approximate measurement with the light meter in a camera; you must translate the photographic readings into footcandles.

Set the film-speed dial to ASA 25 and the shutter speed to 1/60 second. Aim the camera at a sheet of matte white paper or cardboard in the proposed plant location and oriented to the maximum light source. Focus on the paper, getting close enough to it so the meter sees only the white paper. Be sure not to block the light or create a shadow. Adjust the f-stop until the needle is positioned correctly for a picture. Look up the f-stop in the table below to determine approximately how many footcandles there are.

F-stop Setting	Footcandles
2	100
2.8	200
4	370
5.6	750
8	1,500
11	2,800
16	5,000

Using Artificial Light

A greenhouse should get at least six hours of direct sunlight a day. If you were forced to build where the sun cannot reach the green-

Light Requirements

The following list shows the light requirement for many common plants. Low-light plants (L) grow best in 75 to 200 footcandles (f.c.); medium-light plants (M) in 200 to 500 f.c.; and high-light plants (H) in 500 or more f.c. Very high-light plants (VH) need at least 1,000 f.c. but grow best in up to 2,000 f.c.

Aglaonema species (Chinese evergreen) L

Aphelandra squarrosa (zebra plant) M

Araucaria heterophylla (Norfolk Island pine) H

Asparagus densiflorus 'Sprengeri' (Sprenger asparagus) M

Aspidistra elatior (cast-iron plant) L

Aucuba japonica (golddust plant) M

Begonia × rex-cultorum (rex begonia) M

Begonia × semperflorens-cultorum (common begonia) VH

Bougainvillea spectabilis (bougainvillea) VH

Carissa grandiflora (natal plum) H

Chamaerops humilis (European fan palm) H

Chlorophytum comosum (spider plant) H

Chrysanthemum species (chrysanthemum) VH

Cissus antarctica; C. rhombifolia (grape ivy) H

Citrus species (citrus) VH

Codiaeum variegatum var. *pictum* (croton) H

Cordyline terminalis (ti plant) M

Crassula argentea (jade plant) VH

Dianthus caryophyllus (carnation) VH

Dieffenbachia species (dumb cane) M

Dizygotheca elegantissima (false-aralia) M

Dracaena marginata (dragon tree) M

Epipremnum aureum (pothos) L

Eriobotrya japonica (loquat) H

Euonymus japonica (euonymus) M

× *Fatshedera lizei* (tree ivy) M

Fatsia japonica (Japanese aralia) M

Ficus species (ornamental fig) M

Gynura aurantiaca (velvet plant) M

Hedera helix (English ivy) M

Kalanchoe species (kalanchoe) H

Lavandula species (lavender) VH

Maranta leuconeura (prayer plant) M

Opuntia species (prickly pear) VH

Orchids (many species) VH

Pelargonium species (geranium) VH

Pittosporum tobira (mock orange) H

Plectranthus australis (Swedish ivy) M

Rosa species and cultivars (rose) VH

Rosmarinus officinalis (rosemary) VH

Schlumbergera bridgesii (Christmas cactus) H

Tagetes species (marigold) VH

Tradescantia species (wandering Jew) H

It is important to provide greenhouse plants with the amount of light they need for healthy growth. Chrysanthemums require very bright light: between 1,000 and 2,000 footcandles.

house for that length of time, you may need to supplement natural light with artificial light.

In northern climates, where winter days are often short and overcast, many greenhouse gardeners provide plants with needed light by turning on lamps for a couple of hours in the late afternoon. Other gardeners need artificial lights because they like to work in the greenhouse during evening hours.

Incandescent bulbs are the common light bulbs used in the home. The light is rich in red rays but deficient in blue and violet. Incandescents give off a considerable amount of heat, damaging plants growing too close. Generally keep the tops of plants at least 1 foot away from an incandescent source. If your hand feels warm when held at the foliage closest to the light source, the plant is too close.

Fluorescent lamps supply the light most gardeners choose. Although they are somewhat deficient in red, they contain more of the visible light spectrum than incandescents. They are also more efficient, supplying 2½ to 3 times as much light as an incandescent bulb of the same wattage, but only a fraction of the heat. In addition, the lifetime of a fluorescent tube is 15 to 20 times that of an incandescent bulb.

Like incandescents, fluorescents blacken with age and lose light efficiency. Replace them when they reach 70 percent of their stated service life. By that time, they deliver about 15 percent less light than when new.

Since incandescents are deficient in blue rays, and fluorescents are somewhat lacking in red rays, you can combine the two types of lamps so that plants are exposed to the complete spectrum of visible light. The lamps should be mixed at a ratio of one incandescent type to three fluorescent lights of the same wattage.

Manipulating Light

For many plants the relative lengths of night and day determine when they bloom. This phenomenon is known as photoperiodism. By manipulating light and dark in the greenhouse, you can duplicate the natural cycle of plants and force blooming at any time of the year.

Flowering in some plants is triggered by long days and short nights. These long-day plants include petunia, snapdragon, calceolaria, tuberous begonia, bromeliads, azalea, coleus, gloxinia, stephanotis, lily, and hibiscus.

In some other plants flowering is triggered by short days and long nights. These short-day

Left: Fluorescent lamps supply more of the visible light spectrum than incandescent bulbs. Right: Calceolaria blooms when days are long and nights are short. Opposite, top left: Gloxinia is another plant in which blooming is triggered by long days and short nights. Opposite, top right: Rose is a day-neutral plant; blooming does not depend on the length of the day or night. Opposite, bottom: Fuchsia blooms when days are short and nights are long.

plants include aster, fuchsia, gardenia, kalanchoe, chrysanthemum, poinsettia, cattleya orchid, aphelandra, and violet.

Many plants are day-neutral—that is, their blooming is not controlled by the length of days or nights. Among these plants are carnation, cyclamen, rose, wax begonia, and calendula. Blooming depends on other factors, such as temperature, amount of moisture the plant receives, or some genetically determined growth pattern.

The right amount of light and dark stimulates long-day and short-day plants to form flower buds. You can duplicate this natural process in the greenhouse by providing long-day plants with prolonged periods of artificial light approximating the amount of light they would get outdoors in spring or summer when they naturally form flower buds.

You can force short-day plants into bloom by covering them with black cloth to exclude natural light. You give them approximately the same amount of light they get in fall or winter when they normally form flower buds. When shading short-day plants, do it completely as even tiny amounts of light leaking through will prevent flowering.

Building Solar Greenhouses and Sun Pits

You may want to build a solar greenhouse or a sun pit as an alternative to a traditional greenhouse. Depending on the climate and the site, either structure may offer benefits.

A solar greenhouse is worth considering in areas with a high percentage of clear, sunny days. This type of greenhouse is designed to capture the sun's energy and release it at night or on cloudy days to keep the greenhouse warm. In a home greenhouse, a typical heat sink—the thermal mass used to trap and store solar heat—consists of water-filled barrels, piles of rocks, or a concrete or brick wall.

Some hobbyists rely exclusively on solar energy to heat their greenhouses; others combine solar technology with a conventional heating system. Even when used in combination with an electrical or gas heater, solar heat storage principles will help cut energy costs. Pattern your solar greenhouse after one of the two designs shown in this chapter.

The sun pit—a greenhouse sunk below ground level—is another alternative to the traditional greenhouse. Designed to take advantage of the natural insulation of the earth, the sun pit enjoyed popularity during the last century but is an unusual sight today. This type of greenhouse may appeal to you if you have a sunny, well-drained spot for it. You can build one following the plan provided here.

The south wall of this solar greenhouse is angled for maximum exposure to the winter sun. The wood overhang helps shade the greenhouse in summer but has little effect in winter because of the sun's low angle.

Top: Concrete-block planters supplement the concrete-block north wall as a heat sink in this solar greenhouse.
Bottom: Water-filled drums positioned along the north wall are the heat sink in this solar greenhouse shown here and on the previous page.

SOLAR GREENHOUSES

Calling a greenhouse solar is somewhat redundant, since all greenhouses are solar heated to some extent. The greenhouse itself traps the heat each day, as anyone who has been inside a greenhouse for just a few minutes on a sunny day knows. But although a traditional greenhouse acts as a natural solar collector on sunny days, it does not retain the sun's heat at night. Consequently, 75 to 80 percent of the cost of heating a greenhouse by conventional energy sources is expended at night.

To retain the sun's heat, the greenhouse requires something into which the heat can sink and be stored. This heat sink can consist of barrels of water, rocks, concrete walls, or other thermal mass. At night the stored heat emanates back through the greenhouse.

There are two types of solar energy systems: active and passive. The system most commonly used in home greenhouses is passive. Here, a thermal mass, such as rocks or water-filled drums, captures heat during the day and radiates it back at night.

The active system requires electricity or another conventional source of energy to pump heated air into a storage area, such as a basement, filled with rocks or water drums. More efficient than passive solar heating, this type of system is also more expensive and more complex.

Both types of solar systems work better in areas with a high percentage of sunny days, even if they are cold, than they do in areas where overcast days are common.

Solar Heat Storage

Heat arrives from the sun in the form of short waves, which strike and heat objects in the greenhouse. A south-facing greenhouse with a sloping roof permits maximum penetration of sunlight. Inside the greenhouse the heated objects radiate warmth in the form of long waves, which do not readily penetrate the greenhouse covering. These long waves are the ones that can be trapped and stored.

Probably the most widely used heat sink is water in ordinary 55-gallon drums painted a dark, nonreflective color for better heat absorption. Piles of rocks in wire-mesh cages are also common. Place the storage units where they will collect the most heat. Make sure they don't touch the exterior wall or glazing; the outside cold will quickly draw the heat away.

To calculate the minimum heat storage required, allow 2 gallons of water or 80 pounds of rocks for each square foot of greenhouse that admits sunlight directly onto the storage units. Generally, just calculate the south-facing roof and wall.

Another efficient heat sink consists of either a brick wall or cinder blocks poured full of concrete. If you already have an attached greenhouse, cover the back wall—the house wall—with bricks. Buy black bricks or paint them dark for maximum heat absorption. Firmly affix this brick facing to the side of the house with steel braces set in mortar and screwed to the house studs at regular intervals.

The disadvantage of most traditional heat sinks is that they are cumbersome and take up a great deal of space. Newer lightweight materials occupying less space are in the experimental stage. For example, researchers at the University of Delaware are studying solar heat storage in inexpensive chemical compounds known as eutectics. These salts store the heat from the sun's rays at a constant temperature for use on cloudy days and at nights.

Whatever type of heat sink you use in a passive system, you can't count on it to eliminate conventional heating altogether unless your greenhouse operates under ideal conditions. You should have a conventional backup unit ready, although you may not need it very often. You will probably find that the solar heat storage principles put into practice in your greenhouse will help you conserve energy and reduce your heating costs.

Insulation

All the heat you hope to store in your greenhouse will be lost if you can't prevent it from escaping as soon as it is radiated from the heat sink. The greenhouse should be made as airtight as possible. Put weather stripping around the doors and vents, and use a flexible sealant to close all joints between the roof and walls. Make sure the glazing fits snugly.

Even in a tightly sealed greenhouse, heat is lost through the glazing material. The quickest way to cut this loss is to install double or triple glazing, line the interior with inflated layers of polyethylene plastic (see page 38), or use insulating greenhouse curtains that roll down the inside of the glazing at night.

The north wall of the greenhouse provides a quick escape route for heat. You can retain some of that heat by covering the wall with a material that insulates as well as reflects light back into the interior. For an aluminum and glass structure, one effective method is to seal the north wall with panels of white, rigid insulation cut to fit each opening. In a frame greenhouse, you can fill the north wall with fiberglass insulation and cover it with exterior-grade plywood. Apply a coat of water seal to the plywood and then paint it white.

When thinking about insulation, it is easy to forget the floor and foundation. During the winter months in some regions, the ground is frozen many inches deep. That cold surface is a severe drain on greenhouse heat. To block it, put sheets of rigid insulation 1 or 2 inches thick around the outside of the foundation from the footing to the top of the foundation wall. An alternative is to dig a 4-inch-wide trench down to the bottom of the footing and fill it with pumice stone.

The floor—particularly a brick or flagstone floor—is a good heat sink, but its heat gain will be quickly lost if it is not insulated. An effective insulation consists of 4 inches of pumice rock laid beneath the flooring. Water will still drain through.

Solar Heat Sinks

Here are some materials and techniques used for capturing and storing solar heat in greenhouses.

Stacked water-filled steel drums

Water-filled steel drums in metal racks

Concrete-filled cinder or pumice concrete blocks

Brick, stone, or adobe wall

Concrete wall and slab floor

Concrete slab on top of a bed of rocks

Bin or loose pile of rocks

Rock wall held in place with wire-mesh fencing

Passive System

The sun's warmth is deposited and held in the thermal-mass heat sink during the day. At night, this heat radiates out and keeps the greenhouse warm.

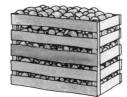

Active System

The sun's heat warms the transfer fluid (water or air) in a solar collector. The fluid is pumped to another location and stored for redistribution as heat later.

Attached Solar Greenhouse

Designed and built by New Mexico landscape architect John Mosely for his own Santa Fe home, the solar greenhouse shown below is attached by a sliding glass door to the house not only for convenience but also to take advantage of greenhouse heat during the winter. In the summer, cooler air in the house is vented through the greenhouse to the outside.

The roof of the 8- by 14-foot glass and redwood structure is angled for maximum exposure to the summer sun. The upper third of the roof is covered with insulation to provide relief from the overhead summer sun.

The 14-foot-wide north wall, made from pumice block poured with concrete, is the heat sink. The outside of the 8-foot-high wall is insulated with 4-inch-thick rigid insulation stuccoed to protect it from the weather.

The front wall and the roof were originally designed to hold only one pane of glass in each opening, but the local code required two. The code also required that the glass windows be separated at the corners, so the block wall was extended and a work area formed beside the outside entrance.

You can adapt this greenhouse to your area, eliminating the block wall extension if it is not required locally. Begin the construction by laying out the site and excavating the ground so that the floor of the greenhouse will be level with the house floor. Position slip forms of 1 by 4s for the footing around the inside perimeter and level them. Form the outside of the footing with rigid insulation braced against the excavated wall. Pour the concrete; when the footing has hardened, build the walls with standard-sized pumice blocks.

Rabbet each vertical stud, plus the top and bottom plates and the crosspieces, to receive the panes of glass. (If you don't have access to a table saw for rabbeting, you can install the glass using quarter-round molding or 1 by 1 redwood strips as stops nailed to the studs and rafters.)

The next step is to frame piece by piece the west wall, which holds the exterior door. The 2 by 6 door frame goes in first. The next elements to be installed are the top plate, the door header, and the window and vent frames.

With the front and side walls in place, it is time to put up the roof. Instead of installing each rafter individually, measure and lay out the roof as if it were a wall. Cut the front end of the rafters so that they are in a vertical line with the front wall. Rabbet each piece as you did the front wall. Then nail together the entire roof section. Lift it into place and toenail it to the top plate of the front wall; nail on a 1 by 6 to cover the seam. With exterior-grade plywood, cover the back area where the roof extended above and slightly over the wall; insulate it inside and outside.

Install the glass, sealing each piece on both sides with butyl rubber. Use 1 by 2 strips to hold the glass in place. Complete the greenhouse by installing a brick-and-sand floor as described on page 32.

Left: The north wall of pumice block and concrete is the heat collector in this attached passive solar greenhouse in Santa Fe.
Right: Landscape architect and owner John Mosely is seen tending the plants in the greenhouse.

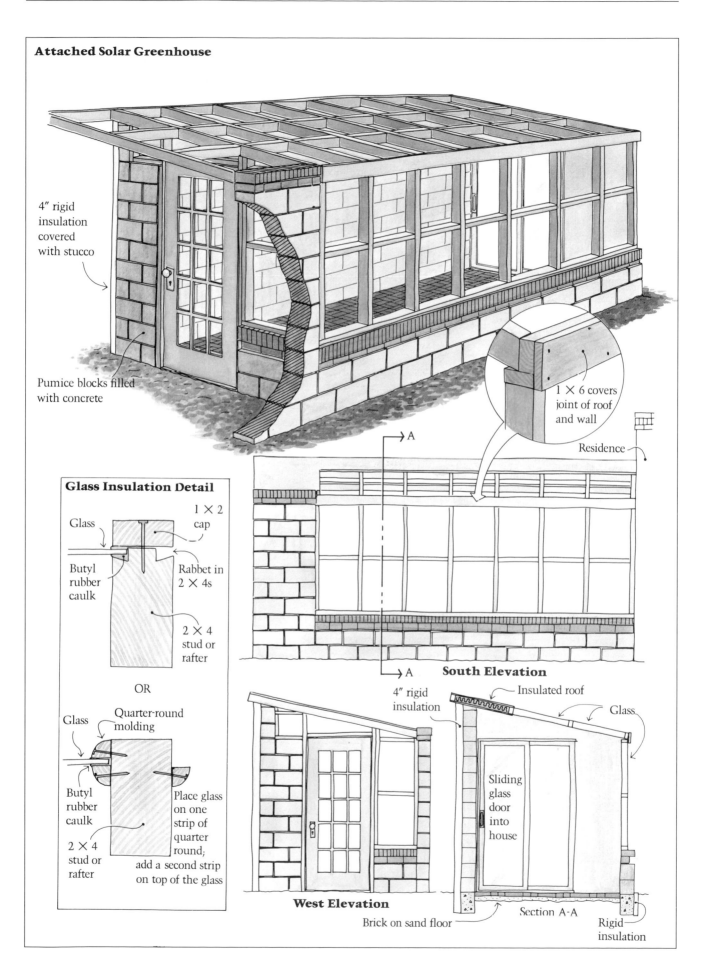

Attached Solar Greenhouse

4" rigid insulation covered with stucco

Pumice blocks filled with concrete

1 × 6 covers joint of roof and wall

Residence

Glass Insulation Detail

Glass

1 × 2 cap

Butyl rubber caulk

Rabbet in 2 × 4s

2 × 4 stud or rafter

OR

Glass

Quarter-round molding

Butyl rubber caulk

2 × 4 stud or rafter

Place glass on one strip of quarter round; add a second strip on top of the glass

South Elevation

A

4" rigid insulation

Insulated roof

Glass

Sliding glass door into house

West Elevation

Brick on sand floor

Section A-A

Rigid insulation

Water-filled drums along the north wall of the greenhouse serve as the solar collector. Planks over the drums provide much-needed bench space.

Angled-Wall Solar Greenhouse

Originally designed by New Mexico builder and solar greenhouse innovator Bill Yanda, the 8-by 12-foot angled-wall structure shown on the opposite page is effective in areas with cold but sunny winters and hot summers. It is similar to the attached model on page 28, except that the south wall is angled to directly face the low winter sun, and the upper portion of the roof is covered and insulated to give some respite inside from the high summer sun.

The angle of the front wall is generally 60 degrees, but another slope may be better for your location. To calculate the optimum angle, put the wall at an angle equal to your geographical latitude plus 35 degrees.

The amount of roof covering also depends on latitude. The covering should be placed to allow the winter sun to strike high on the back wall, which absorbs and stores heat. Although the covering shades about one third of the greenhouse in the summer, there is still enough reflected light for good growing. Move heat- and sun-loving plants to the front of the greenhouse during the summer months.

Once the foundation and sill are in place (see pages 20 to 26), the next step is to build the front wall. In this model, the south wall and roof have studs and rafters at intervals of 2 feet on center.

Before laying out the wall, cut the studs at the angle you wish. For a 60-degree slope, use a protractor to make a 30-degree angle on the bottom of the stud. The angle of the cut is always the difference between the vertical of 90 degrees and the angle you want the wall to be. Cut the top of the stud parallel to the bottom so the top plate will lie flat. When the studs are cut, lay out the wall. Nail the wall together, and put it in place with bracing at both ends.

The next step is to put up the rafters. If you can bolt them to the overhang on your house, that is satisfactory. Otherwise, put up a 2 by 6 ledger board, 12 feet long, on the house and support each rafter with a joist hanger. You can eliminate the expense of joist hangers by notching each rafter 1¼ to 1½ inches, depending on the thickness of the ledger. Fit the notched rafters over the ledger board and toenail them into place.

For the front of the rafter to lie flat on the wall plate, you must cut bird's mouth openings. Hold one rafter in place at the outside end of the wall, and mark the required angle of cut. Use this rafter as a pattern for cutting the remaining rafters. When all are cut, toenail them into place directly over the wall studs.

Now measure the front third—more or less, depending on geographical latitude—of the roof rafters. Then snap a chalk line across the rafters. This line indicates where the clear and opaque portions of the roof will meet. Nail 2 by 4 bracings straight across on this line.

Before proceeding any further, put the end walls in place. The top plate on the end walls ties directly into the front wall plate. From this junction, run a stud down to the bottom plate. On the end where the door will be located, use two studs nailed together on the side of the

Angled-Wall Solar Greenhouse

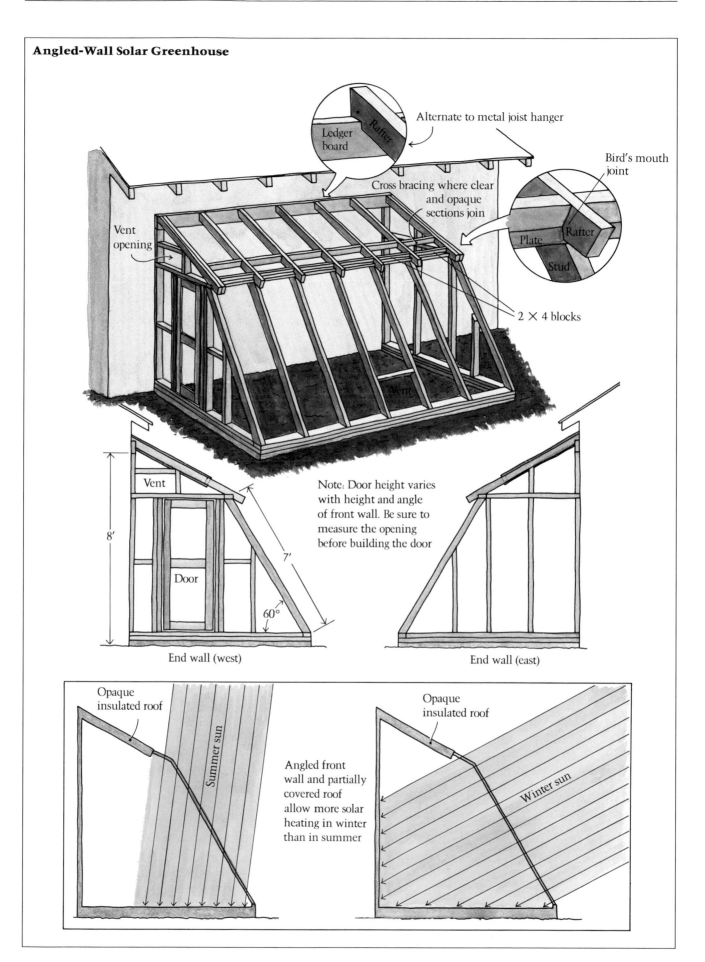

Alternate to metal joist hanger

Ledger board

Rafter

Cross bracing where clear and opaque sections join

Bird's mouth joint

Plate

Rafter

Stud

Vent opening

2 × 4 blocks

Vent

Vent

Door

8'

7'

60°

End wall (west)

Note: Door height varies with height and angle of front wall. Be sure to measure the opening before building the door

End wall (east)

Opaque insulated roof

Summer sun

Opaque insulated roof

Winter sun

Angled front wall and partially covered roof allow more solar heating in winter than in summer

Top: The walls of the angled-wall solar greenhouse are built on the ground, then raised when ready to connect together. The studs and rafters are spaced 2 feet apart, on center.
Center: Corrugated fiberglass is being lifted onto the roof.
Bottom: Flat fiberglass is used for the side and front walls.

opening where the hinges will go. Measure off the door opening, allowing ¼ inch additional space for clearance, and put in the other side of the door frame. This stud should be cross-braced midway up the wall to either the adjoining stud or to the end wall stud that is tied to the house.

On the front wall between each rafter, nail in a 2 by 4 so it is flush with the top of the rafters. You may have to use a rip saw for an even, tight fit. Next, cover all crosspieces on the roof with strips of corrugated foam, redwood, or rubber molding. You are almost ready to install the corrugated roof panels.

First, drill the nail holes in each panel. Along the top edge, which will be covered by the solid portion of the roof, drill holes in every third ridge of the corrugation. Along the bottom, which will be pulled at by the wind, drive in an aluminum nail with a neoprene washer in every ridge.

Now, across the upper edge of the fiberglass roof, lay in another strip of molding right on top of the fiberglass, and add a bead of sealant. Then put the solid panels of ⅜-inch exterior-grade plywood in place. To keep the rain from blowing in, allow the plywood to overlap the fiberglass by 4 inches. As an alternative, you can use corrugated steel for the opaque portion of the roof; although steel is difficult to vent, it will mesh with the corrugated fiberglass.

If the back of the roof is not under an overhang, metal flashing must be used between it and the house. In any event, this area must be tightly sealed. The plywood can then be covered with composition or cedar shingles, or it can be painted.

On the front and side walls, use flat fiberglass panels. Before nailing each panel, put down a bead of sealant and make sure the panel is square. Drive in flat-head galvanized 4d nails every 6 inches. When all the pieces are installed, lay another bead of sealant along the joints and cover the joints with a strip of redwood lath.

Staple fiberglass insulation to the solid roof inside, and cover it with wood or paneling of your choice. Paint the whole interior of the greenhouse, including the solid roof section, white to reflect light back into the greenhouse. Finally, to create the dead-air insulating barrier, cover the interior with 4-mil, ultraviolet-resistant polyethylene plastic film.

SUN PITS

A sun-heated pit greenhouse, which is sunk below ground and has a roof sitting at ground level, is often likened to a walk-in cold frame. The roof may be an A-frame, or it may be rounded or arched. Once a familiar sight, the structure is a rarity today. It has disadvantages as well as advantages, and you must weigh the two before deciding to build a sun pit.

The sun pit requires little or no external heating, especially if it is used as a cool greenhouse. It takes advantage of the natural insulation of the ground and suffers little heat loss through the walls to the soil. Its low profile protects it from the wind.

Its main disadvantages are the cost of excavation (a backhoe is usually needed), the difficulty in heating and ventilating the structure, the inability to wheel soil right up to the benches, and water washing in during heavy rainstorms.

Sun Pit Construction

When constructing a sun pit, the main factors to consider are sunlight and drainage. The sun pit should be positioned so that the length of the roof faces south. Attending to drainage is important with a sunken structure like a sun pit; if you neglect it at the beginning, you may find yourself working in mud and water later, when little can be done to rectify the situation.

Allow as much room as possible for the sun pit. An 8- by 12-foot structure is the bare minimum, according to many sun pit owners. A 12- by 18-foot structure will give you growing space on both sides of the pit and down the middle.

The pit should be 4 feet deep, regardless of the dimensions. Once it is dug, square the sides until they are vertical, and level the floor. Around the edge, dig a ditch 4 inches deep and 12 inches wide for the footing, which should be poured with the aid of leveling stakes as described on page 23. Also dig a sump 30 inches

Sunk below ground, the sun pit takes advantage of the natural insulation of the earth. Although a sunken structure may have some drawbacks, such as possible flooding during heavy rainstorms, with careful management it can make a satisfactory home greenhouse.

deep and about 18 inches wide from which irrigation and seepage water can be pumped out of the pit. While waiting for the footing to dry, dig the steps at the end away from prevailing winter winds. Now is also the time to bring in water and electrical lines.

When the footing has cured, start laying the concrete-block wall. Insulate it on the outside with 1-inch-thick rigid insulation.

When erecting the foundation wall, instead of mortaring each block in place, lay a course of blocks and then fill every other opening with concrete and tamp thoroughly. Once the concrete has stiffened, lay another course and fill the alternate holes. Keep checking the level and plumb of the wall as you go.

The next step is to finish the flooring while you can still get a wheelbarrow in. At this depth, the ground is relatively warm and insulation under the floor is not necessary. Either brick on sand or 4 inches of pea gravel make a good floor. You may decide to put the gravel under the benches, and to cover the walkways with brick on sand.

Once the flooring and the water and electrical connections have been installed, you're ready to start the roof. For the conventional A-frame style, start by erecting a 2 by 6 ridge board directly down the center of the pit. It should be about 8 feet above the floor.

To find the angle of end cuts so the rafters fit smoothly against the ridge board and the sills, hold one rafter in place at the end, mark it, and use it as a pattern for the other rafters. For a 12-foot-long sun pit, cut 18 rafters and place them 2 feet on center doubling up the end rafters to provide a good nailing surface for the end walls. Vent openings should be placed in each end wall directly under the ridge.

For a sun pit without electrically operated fans, install vent openings on the north slope of the roof near the peak. Space the vents at every other rafter opening.

Cover the north slope of the roof with ½-inch plywood topped with 90-pound roofing felt and then with shingles or other weatherproof covering. Inside, staple 3-inch fiberglass insulation between the studs and cover it with 3-inch exterior-grade plywood. Paint the ceiling white to reflect light onto the plants.

Cover the south wall with 4-foot-wide sheets of corrugated fiberglass. Fit top and bottom of each panel over corrugated foam molding and nail through every other ridge. Cover ridge of roof with an aluminum roof cap, remembering to put down another layer of foam molding between it and the fiberglass for a tight seal.

Cover the end walls with glass set between the stud openings or with flat fiberglass. In cold-winter areas, insulate the end walls.

Mixing Concrete

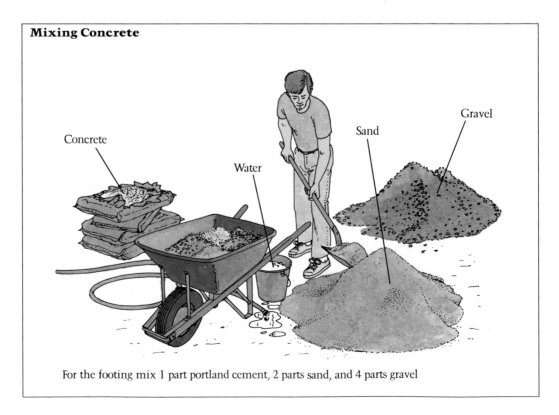

For the footing mix 1 part portland cement, 2 parts sand, and 4 parts gravel

Sun Pit

Detail of South Half of Roof

Aluminum roof cap

Corrugated molding

Corrugated fiberglass

Corrugated molding at top and bottom of roof and on any cross bracing

Detail of North Half of Roof

Shingles

90 lb. roofing felt

½" exterior-grade plywood

3" fiberglass insulation between rafters

⅜" exterior-grade plywood

Vents at each end

Sill attached to concrete blocks with anchor bolts (see pages 22 and 26)

Stairs minimum 3′ wide (railroad ties make excellent stairs)

Brick on sand floor for central aisle

Concrete-block wall

Pea gravel floor under benches

Concrete footing

Rigid insulation 1″ thick

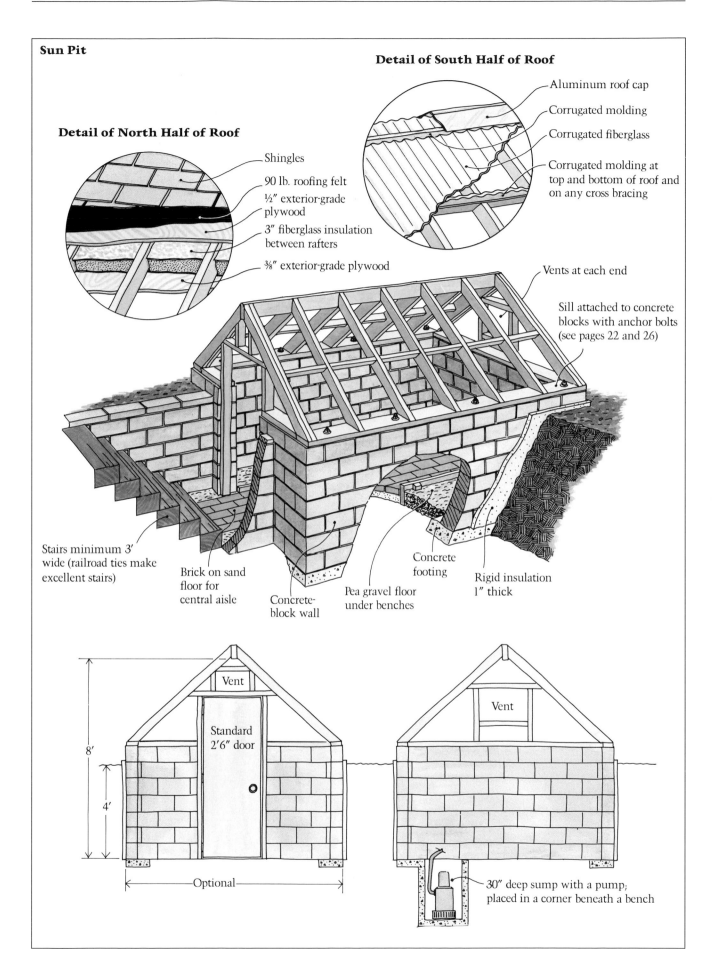

Vent

Standard 2′6″ door

8′

4′

Optional

Vent

30″ deep sump with a pump; placed in a corner beneath a bench

Using Your Greenhouse

After the greenhouse has been built and outfitted, it is time to put it to use. Greenhouse growing projects you may want to try include propagating plants and experimenting with hydroponics.

A new greenhouse is like a clean slate; the stamp you place upon it is limited only by your preferences, imagination, and available time.

One of the best uses for a greenhouse is plant propagation. The warm, moist environment is ideal for starting new plants from seeds and cuttings. Your goal may be to inexpensively produce large quantities of plants for your garden. Or, you may want to focus on a particular group of plants and become a specialty plant collector and propagator. A good resource is a plant society whose members share your interest; consider joining one or more societies listed in this chapter. Also included are directions for building a seed-starting chamber (see page 99) and a mist propagation bench (see page 104), both of which will improve your chances of success as a greenhouse propagator.

For the adventurous, the greenhouse is an excellent place in which to experiment with hydroponics. Gardeners converted to soilless growing—and they number in the thousands—claim that their vegetables grow faster and taste better than those grown in traditional gardens. Included are directions for building a basic hydroponic system (see page 106) that takes up little space.

The greenhouse is also a good place to teach children—either your own or someone else's—about the joys of growing and caring for plants. Included in this chapter are projects that educate as well as amuse.

Most greenhouse gardeners find propagating plants from cuttings and seeds immensely satisfying. A corner of this greenhouse is devoted to propagation.

Left: Easily started from seed, impatiens germinates in about 15 days at 70° F (21° C). Do not bury the seeds. Right: A seedling should be moved to its pot after it develops four true leaves.

PROPAGATING FROM SEEDS

One of the things you will like best about your greenhouse is being able to grow many of the plants for your garden from seed. Because a greenhouse can provide the moisture and warmth needed for germination, it is an ideal place for starting seeds.

When propagating seeds, keep in mind that each seed is the unique genetic product of the parent plants, and the resulting plant can vary slightly or dramatically from its parents. Seeds saved from your garden plants, if they are hybrids, may revert unpredictably to a parent and may not develop into the form you expect. However, seeds sold commercially have a predictable form when grown.

Most vegetables and many flowers are very easy to grow from seed. Some seeds are more difficult to handle than others and require special treatment before they will germinate. For example, some seeds have a very hard seed coat that must be gently scraped or nicked so that moisture can enter to trigger the germination process. Other seeds must be chilled to induce germination. Seeds that contain a chemical inhibitor must be soaked before they will sprout. Still other seeds must be subjected to either complete darkness or exposed to light before germination will take place.

Most seeds can be sown in large flats and then moved into individual pots or into the ground; some plants that resist transplanting should be sown in their own pots. Use a sterile medium. A good choice is horticultural-grade vermiculite or a potting mix such as one containing perlite, vermiculite, and sphagnum peat moss.

Most seeds do best when barely covered. Be sure not to cover seeds that need light for germination. If darkness is required, bury the seeds if they are fairly large; if they are very fine, block the light with cardboard.

The length of time until germination depends on the plant species. The seeds of some plants germinate in as few as five days; others, such as parsley, may take three weeks. The seed contains stored food, so it is not necessary to fertilize until the first true set of leaves (the seed leaves are called cotyledons) appear.

After a seedling has developed four true leaves, it should be moved into its own pot. You may want to move the young plant one more time into a larger container. Once it develops a healthy root system, you can plant it in a permanent spot.

Seed-Starting Chamber

Constant warmth is necessary for successful seed germination. Since there is no need to keep the entire greenhouse warm, especially during the night, you will want to confine seed germination to a small area. In effect, you need to build a miniature greenhouse inside your greenhouse.

A seed-starting chamber is easy and very inexpensive to construct. It consists of a wooden frame, plastic sheeting, seed flats, water pans, and a heating cable.

Nail four 1 by 4s together to form a frame that covers a portion of one of your benches. Then stretch a sheet of clear polyethylene film over the top of the frame, overlapping all sides so that you can staple it. In the bench section where you want the chamber, lay the heating cable. The loops should not touch, but instead should run back and forth so that they are about 3 or 4 inches apart.

Cover the cable with 1 inch of sand or a sterile potting mix. Also bury the thermostat. Set one or more leakproof pans over the buried heating cable. If you do not have the right size pans for your flats, you may want to make some from sheet metal. These pans will provide subirrigation to keep the seeds moist, hastening their germination. Drying out can be fatal to germinating seeds, so the pans must hold enough water to keep the seed-starting medium moist at all times. Fill the seed flats with a sterile medium suitable for starting seeds. In these you will sow the seeds.

Keep a thermometer inside the chamber so that you can monitor the temperature. Most seeds need 70° to 75° F (21° to 24° C); some, including parsley, verbena, pansy, phlox, and cornflower, prefer 65° F (18° C). If the temperature climbs too high during hot days, simply raise the frame by propping open one side. Be sure to let it down at night. On a cold, windy night, you may need to throw a plastic sheet over the whole chamber to keep out drafts.

Soon after the seeds are showing green, move them out of the germinating bed into a sheltered part of the greenhouse. They will do well in temperatures as low as 50° F (10° C).

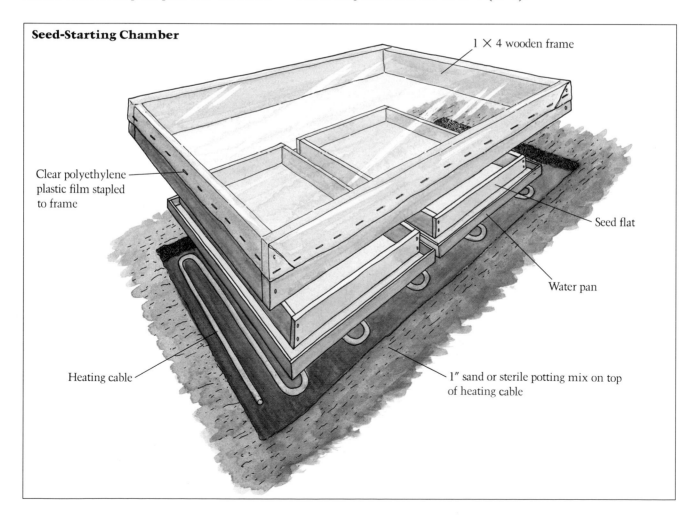

Seed-Starting Chamber

1 × 4 wooden frame

Clear polyethylene plastic film stapled to frame

Seed flat

Water pan

Heating cable

1″ sand or sterile potting mix on top of heating cable

Seed Germination

	Best Germinating Temperature	Light or Darkness Needed	Number of Days for Germination	Time to Start Indoors for Outdoor Planting
Ageratum houstonianum (flossflower)	70° F (21° C)	Light	5	12–16 weeks
Alcea rosea (hollyhock)	60° F (16° C)	Either	10	12–16 weeks
Alyssum species	70° F (21° C)	Either	5	12–16 weeks
Antirrhinum majus (snapdragon)	70° F (21° C)	Light	10	12–14 weeks
Begonia species (fibrous rooted)	70° F (21° C)	Light	15	18–22 weeks
Browallia speciosa (amethyst flower)	70° F (21° C)	Light	15	12–16 weeks
Calendula officinalis (pot marigold)	70° F (21° C)	Dark	10	4–6 weeks
Callistephus chinensis (annual aster)	70° F (21° C)	Either	15	4–6 weeks
Catharanthus roseus (periwinkle)	70° F (21° C)	Dark	15	10–12 weeks
Celosia species (cockscomb)	70° F (21° C)	Either	10	6–8 weeks
Centaurea cineraria (dusty-miller)	70° F (21° C)	Light	10	12–14 weeks
Centaurea cyanus (cornflower)	65° F (18° C)	Dark	10	8–10 weeks
Coleus species	70° F (21° C)	Light	10	8–10 weeks
Cosmos species	70° F (21° C)	Either	5	6–8 weeks
Dahlia species	70° F (21° C)	Either	5	10–12 weeks
Dianthus caryophyllus (carnation)	70° F (21° C)	Either	20	12–16 weeks
Dianthus species (pinks)	70° F (21° C)	Either	5	12–16 weeks
Gaillardia pulchella (annual blanket-flower)	70° F (21° C)	Either	20	12–16 weeks
Heliotropium arborescens (heliotrope)	70° F (21° C)	Either	25	10–12 weeks
Impatiens species	70° F (21° C)	Light	15	9–12 weeks
Lathyrus odoratus (sweet pea)	55° F (13° C)	Dark	15	8–10 weeks
Lobelia species	70° F (21° C)	Either	20	15–22 weeks
Nicotiana alata (flowering tobacco)	70° F (21° C)	Light	20	4–6 weeks
Nierembergia hippomanica (cupflower)	70° F (21° C)	Either	15	10–12 weeks
Pelargonium species (geranium)	75° F (24° C)	Either	5–10	18–20 weeks
Petunia hybrids	70° F (21° C)	Light	10	10–15 weeks
Phlox drummondii (annual phlox)	65° F (18° C)	Dark	10	8–12 weeks
Portulaca species (moss-pink)	70° F (21° C)	Dark	15	6–8 weeks
Rudbeckia species (coneflower)	70° F (21° C)	Either	10	10–12 weeks
Salvia splendens (annual sage)	70° F (21° C)	Light	15	8–14 weeks
Tagetes species (marigold)	70° F (21° C)	Either	5	6–10 weeks
Verbena species	65° F (18° C)	Dark	20	8–10 weeks
Viola × *wittrockiana* (pansy)	65° F (18° C)	Dark	10	22–26 weeks
Zinnia species	70° F (21° C)	Either	5	4–6 weeks

PROPAGATING FROM CUTTINGS

Propagating from cuttings—portions of stems, leaves, or roots—is a quick, economical way to produce large quantities of plants. Some plants are started from cuttings because their seeds may take many years to grow into full-sized plants. Most fruit and nut trees and many ornamental shrubs are propagated this way because they may not grow true (similar in form to their parents) when started from seed.

Many plants reproduce easily from cuttings. Usually the cuttings are taken from stems, although some plants reproduce better from leaf or root cuttings.

The rooting medium can consist of almost any sterile mix that drains well yet retains moisture. Many greenhouse gardeners like a combination of perlite, vermiculite, and ground sphagnum peat moss. Others prefer using perlite or vermiculite alone, or with a small amount of peat moss added. Don't add fertilizer until you transplant the rooted cuttings.

Commercial rooting hormones can benefit some plants, but many plants produce enough hormones on their own. (The hormone compounds available commercially are organic and rather unstable. Store them in a closed container and away from light, preferably in a freezer.) If the bottom of a cutting is turning black, chances are that the rooting hormone is too strong.

The trays of cuttings should be exposed to bright light (about 600 to 2,000 footcandles) and a temperature between 65° and 70° F (18° to 21° C). The surrounding air can be cooler if you have a heating cable that keeps the bottom of the propagation bed 70° to 75° F (21° to 24° C). Mist the cuttings once or twice a day.

Stem Cuttings

These are the most common types of cuttings. The principle behind stem cuttings is that, given the right conditions, a piece of stem with buds will develop roots and grow into a new plant. There are four major categories of stem cuttings: hardwood, semihardwood, softwood, and herbaceous.

Hardwood cuttings   Cuttings are considered to be hardwood when they come from shoots that have grown through an entire season, and the plant from which the cuttings are taken is either dormant or approaching a dormant period. The plant cells are fully formed and lignification—strengthening into woody tissue—has taken place. Of all the types of cuttings, hardwood cuttings are the least likely to dry out or succumb to disease.

How you handle hardwood cuttings depends on whether they come from deciduous plants or narrow-leaved evergreens.

Deciduous plants   Many, although not all, deciduous flowering shrubs can be propagated from stem cuttings taken in the fall, just after the leaves have dropped. Use shoots that grew during the spring and summer of that year.

Discard the top 10 or 12 inches of each shoot because this wood is not likely to be fully mature. Cut the remaining wood into 12-inch lengths. Distinguish the top from the base by cutting the top straight across and the bottom at a slant. Each length should have several nodes—the junctures where the leaves were joined to the stem. Discard those that don't. Scratch or slice the bark 2 or 3 inches from the bottom, and rub a little rooting hormone compound into these wounds.

Bundle about 10 to 25 cuttings, bottom ends in the same direction. Tie each bundle loosely and label it. Pack the bundles, bottom ends up, in a 5-gallon or other container that is 5 or 6

Taking Cuttings

Keep in mind these general rules when taking cuttings from plants.
• The younger the cutting, the more likely it is to establish roots. Cuttings from most plants should be taken from shoots that are less than a year old. There are a few exceptions, such as olives, that may do better if the cutting is from second-year wood.
• The nearer the root the young cutting is taken, the better the chances that it, in turn, will take root.
• The larger the mature size of a plant, the less likely a cutting will take root. There are exceptions to this rule—for example, cuttings from poplar and willow trees root fairly easily. Experts have even been able to reproduce the coast redwood, which towers hundreds of feet tall in forests, from cuttings.
• The more leaves on a cutting, the better it will root because some of the most important plant hormones are produced in the margins of the leaves and at the growing points of the foliage. However, too much foliage causes the cutting to lose more moisture than it can take in. Consequently, the cutting will dry out.
• The more light the cutting gets, the faster it will root. This is because photosynthesis speeds up, and more sugars are produced to fuel growth. Of course, too much direct, hot sunlight damages cuttings.

Softwood and herbaceous stem cuttings should be taken just below a node (where the leaves join the stem). Strip off the lower leaves before inserting the cuttings in the rooting medium.

Left: Rhododendron is usually propagated from semihardwood cuttings. A good time to take cuttings is about 30 days after flowering.
Sequence for propagating cuttings (clockwise):
Top center: Make each cutting approximately 4 inches long, and remove the lower leaves.
Top right: Cut off the tops of the remaining leaves, and make a lengthwise slice with a knife or razor blade at the base of each cutting to expose the inner wood.
Bottom right: Dip the base of each stem into a rooting hormone.
Bottom center: Insert the stems into a rooting mix consisting of equal parts clean sand, peat, and perlite.

inches deeper than the cuttings and has drainage holes. Placing them upside down promotes root irritation and slows down the development of buds. Fill the container with coarse perlite, set it in a cool place away from the light—under a bench is a good place—and water it once or twice a week.

If you take the cuttings in November or December, they should be well healed and ready to plant by mid-February. Plant the cuttings, top end up, in pots or trays about 6 or 8 inches deep and 6 inches apart, and put them in a cool place with plenty of light. As the weather warms and the days get brighter, move the containers to a shady location outside. By July or August the young shrubs will be ready for planting in the garden.

Narrow-leaved evergreens These cuttings are slow to root, often taking many months or even a year. Some—including yew, juniper, arborvitae, cypress, and some cedars and pines—are among the easiest to root. Generally, the lower-growing species are easier to propagate than the taller, upright ones.

Take shoots from the past season's growth, discard a few inches of the less mature wood at the tip, and cut the rest into lengths of approximately 4 inches. Dip the lower half of each cutting in a rooting hormone, and plant the cuttings about 2½ inches deep in perlite. If you have a heating cable, set it at 65° to 75° F (18° to 24° C) and place the container of planted cuttings on it. Water daily.

In 10 to 16 weeks, most of the cuttings should be rooted, but wait patiently if they're not. Move the rooted cuttings either into pots or into a transplant bed, leaving 6 inches between cuttings. Leave them there for the first summer, watering and feeding them at regular intervals; they can be transplanted to their permanent locations during either the second or third summer.

Semihardwood cuttings These are cuttings from broadleaf evergreen plants, such as holly, viburnum, rhododendron, and camellia. Leafy summer cuttings from partially mature wood of deciduous plants can also be considered semihardwood. (When taken in the fall after leaves drop, the cuttings are hardwood.)

Semihardwood cuttings are perhaps the most difficult to handle. The biggest problem is figuring out when the wood is at the right maturity. If the tip of the branch snaps when you bend it, the wood is probably too mature. If it bends double without breaking, it's probably not old enough and will start to wilt as soon as you put it in the rooting mix. You can usually find the right maturity by experimenting. Take a few cuttings from the tips of branches every week and watch for rooting.

Try to choose shoots that are plump and have full-sized leaves. If the species has large leaves, cut some of them in half. Follow the rooting procedure described above for narrow-leaved evergreens. The rooted cuttings need protection during their first winter; keep them in the greenhouse or in a cold frame.

Softwood cuttings Taken from soft, new spring growth of deciduous or evergreen woody plants, softwood cuttings are the quickest of all to root, usually in two to five weeks. They are also quick to die if not given the right conditions. Among the plants commonly propagated from softwood cuttings are forsythia, magnolia, spirea, and maple.

Softwood cuttings should be taken early in the day and rooted as soon as possible before they have a chance to dry out. Side branches, rather than terminal branches, generally provide the best cuttings. A softwood cutting should be 3 to 5 inches long and should have two or more nodes. Make the bottom cut just under a node. Strip off the bottom leaves. If the cutting has many or very large leaves on the upper portion, remove some or cut them down in size; also remove any flowers or flower buds.

Dip each cutting in a rooting hormone and insert it to half its length in the rooting medium. Maintain high humidity and bottom heat of 75° to 80° F (24° to 27° C). Water and fertilize the cuttings regularly.

Herbaceous cuttings These are taken from herbaceous plants (those with soft rather than woody stems) such as chrysanthemum, geranium, and fibrous begonia.

Herbaceous cuttings are usually 3 to 5 inches long. Treat them as you would softwood cuttings. As soon as they are well rooted, they can be transplanted directly into the garden.

Cuttings from plants that exude a sticky sap—for example, cactus and geranium—should be air-dried so that the cutting wounds start to heal before you plant. Geranium cuttings should be exposed to the air, but not to the sun, for about half a day; cuttings from cactus and other succulents require two or three days. After planting, be careful not to overwater a succulent; once every week or two is enough.

Leaf cuttings Some plants, such as African violets, begonias, and many succulents, will root from a leaf or part of a leaf. Most plants that possess this ability are characterized by thick fleshy stems and leaves covered with fine hairs.

Top: Leaf cuttings of African violet root easily. Bottom: Schefflera can be propagated by leaf-bud cuttings. The cutting consists of a leaf and a short piece of the stem with an attached bud.

Choose recently mature leaves for the cuttings. How the leaf is handled depends on the plant. In some cases, you will cut the main veins on the underside of the leaf and lay the leaf flat on the rooting medium; in other cases, you will insert the leaves upright into the rooting medium. A good medium for rooting leaf cuttings is half perlite and half sphagnum peat moss. Maintain high humidity, and lightly fertilize after a week or 10 days.

Begonias will root from a leaf petiole, or leafstalk. They will also root from breaks in the veins of a leaf if it is laid flat on the rooting mix and pegged down with a toothpick. When two little leaves have formed on the parent leaf, look for tiny rows of red or black spots on the underside indicating where the roots will grow. This part of the leaf should be inserted ¼ inch into the rooting medium.

African violets and gloxinias also root easily, although they take a little longer than begonias. Drops of cold water will blemish their leaves, so be careful when watering, and don't expose them to mist.

Some philodendrons can be easily rooted from a leaf that includes a bit of the branch it was attached to. Sometimes this is called a mallet or club cutting. Be sure not to plant this type of cutting more than 1½ inches deep.

Root cuttings   Almost any plant species that has two or more stems emerging from the ground can be reproduced from root cuttings. This is an especially good method for propagating lilac and quince, which aren't easily rooted from stem cuttings.

The best time to take root cuttings is just before an active period of growth, usually very early spring. Dig up the plant or part of it to get the cuttings, then replant it.

Cut 3- or 4-inch lengths of root taken from just below ground. Plant them in rows about ¼ inch below the surface of the rooting medium. Some species can be placed horizontally whereas others must be planted vertically. When planting vertically, place the cuttings top end up. Cut the top straight and the bottom at a slant when taking the cuttings.

Keep the cuttings watered, and a few weeks later you should see shoots emerging.

Mist Propagation Bench

The best place for rooting cuttings is a mist propagation bench. Simple and relatively inexpensive to construct, it will become a useful addition to your greenhouse.

The mist propagation bench should be made of a material impervious to water. A good choice is rot-resistant wood lined with polyethylene film plastic and covered with a 1-inch base of gravel and a 2-inch top of perlite or washed sand from a lumberyard. This setup is excellent for rooting cuttings in flats or trays. If you want to root directly into the bench, add another 2 inches of perlite or vermiculite, or use a mixture of the two.

Since misting tends to lower the soil temperature, the growing medium should be heated with electric cables. During the summer, bottom heat may not be necessary.

Usually, a ¾-inch PVC pipe is adequate to conduct water to the bench. The pipe can either be suspended overhead or built into the bench. Either way, the spray nozzles should be about 18 inches above the cuttings.

The spacing of the misters depends on their radius of throw; follow the manufacturer's directions carefully. To cover all areas of the bench, you must overlap the sprays slightly.

Mist Propagation Bench

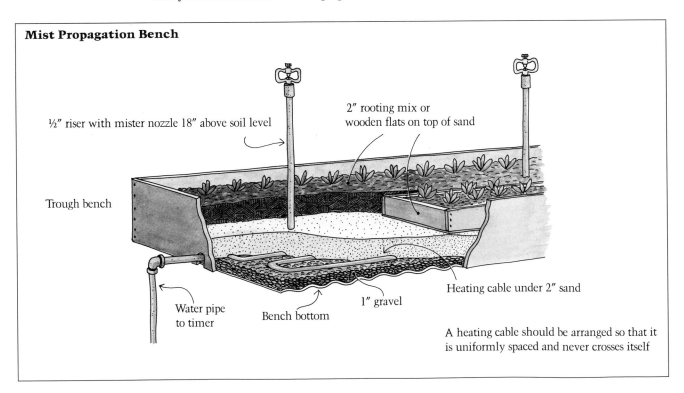

½" riser with mister nozzle 18" above soil level

2" rooting mix or wooden flats on top of sand

Trough bench

Heating cable under 2" sand

Water pipe to timer

Bench bottom

1" gravel

A heating cable should be arranged so that it is uniformly spaced and never crosses itself

These attractive wooden hydroponic growing beds contain tomato vines as well as ornamental plants.

Plant Societies

Joining one or more plant societies will help you get even more mileage from your greenhouse investment. Members are generally very knowledgeable, and they often write helpful articles based on personal experience.

African Violet Society of America
Box 3609
Beaumont, TX 77704

American Begonia Society
8922 Conway Drive
Riverside, CA 92503

American Fern Society
Department of Botany
University of Tennessee
Knoxville, TN 37996

American Fuchsia Society
County Fair Building
Ninth Avenue at Lincoln Way
San Francisco, CA 94122

American Gloxinia and Gesneriad Society
Box 493
Beverly Farms, MA 01915

American Orchid Society
6000 South Olive Avenue
West Palm Beach, FL 33405

Bromeliad Society, Inc.
2488 East 49th Street
Tulsa, OK 74105

Cactus and Succulent Society of America
Box 3010
Santa Barbara, CA 93130

Cymbidium Society of America
6881 Wheeler Avenue
Westminster, CA 92683

Hobby Greenhouse Association
4862 U.S. Route 68 North
Yellow Springs, OH 45387

Hoya Society International
Box 54271
Atlanta, GA 30308

Hydroponic Society of America
Box 6067
Concord, CA 94553

Indoor Gardening Society of America
5305 Southwest Hamilton Street
Portland, OR 97221

International Geranium Society
4610 Druid Street
Los Angeles, CA 90032

Los Angeles International Fern Society
Box 90943
Pasadena, CA 91109

National Chrysanthemum Society
10107 Homar Pond Drive
Fairfax Station, VA 22039

Saintpaulia International
1650 Cherry Hill Road
State College, PA 16803

Terrarium Association
Box 276
Newfane, VT 05345

HYDROPONIC GROWING

Hydroponics is simply the cultivation of plants in a nutrient solution rather than in soil. A water solution rich with nutrients is washed or pumped through a light gravel or other medium that anchors the plants and retains the solution. The process is also known as aquaculture, nutriculture, and hydroculture.

Growing hydroponically is easier today than it was when it became popular decades ago. Instead of having to mix your own nutrient solution from chemicals, you can now purchase premixed water-soluble fertilizers containing the full range of nutrients for healthy plant growth. These fertilizers are readily available in nurseries and garden supply centers.

The traditional hydroponic medium is pea gravel, although it is heavy and must be hosed to remove any soil or clay. Washed sand from a lumberyard is also acceptable, but it is heavy and slow to drain. Perlite and vermiculite have the advantage of being sterile and lightweight; they both hold water well, although vermiculite may retain too much. The newest aggregate to be used in hydroponic beds is rock wool, an inert, sterile material made by blowing steam through molten rock; it holds air and water well. Wood chips and sawdust are the last resort, but they can serve as a medium if given sufficient amounts of nitrogen; make sure the wood used isn't toxic to plants.

The core of any hydroponic system, whether simple or complex, is a leakproof growing bed that fills and drains rapidly. You can purchase a ready-made unit, or you can build your own. Instructions for building a basic one are given on the next page.

Basic Hydroponic Bed

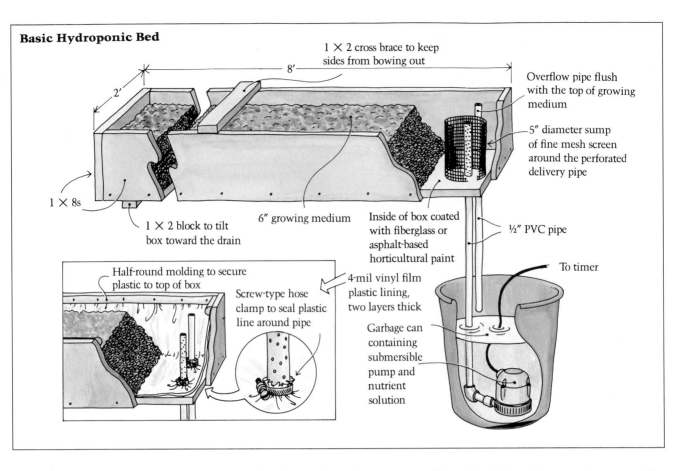

1 × 2 cross brace to keep sides from bowing out

8'

2'

Overflow pipe flush with the top of growing medium

5" diameter sump of fine mesh screen around the perforated delivery pipe

1 × 8s

1 × 2 block to tilt box toward the drain

6" growing medium

Inside of box coated with fiberglass or asphalt-based horticultural paint

½" PVC pipe

To timer

Half-round molding to secure plastic to top of box

Screw-type hose clamp to seal plastic line around pipe

4-mil vinyl film plastic lining, two layers thick

Garbage can containing submersible pump and nutrient solution

Detailed information about hydroponics can be obtained from the Hydroponic Society of America, Box 6067, Concord, CA 94553.

Basic Hydroponic System

You can make a simple, inexpensive hydroponic growing bed for your greenhouse. Automating the system with a small electric pump and timer will ensure that twice-daily feedings aren't missed.

Begin by nailing together 1 by 8s to form a box 8 feet long and 2 feet wide. Use a sheet of exterior-grade plywood for the bottom of the box. Nail a 1 by 2 strip across the top center to prevent the sides from bowing out.

Glue all the joints with epoxy glue, and caulk the seams. Line the box with two layers of 4-mil film plastic. Anywhere a pipe enters the box, gather a little of the plastic around the pipe, and use a screw-type hose clamp to make it tight and leak resistant.

Deliver the nutrient solution to the bed through a perforated pipe about 6 inches long and protected from the growing medium by a sump of wire mesh. The wire mesh allows you to clean the holes in the pipe periodically without digging up the medium.

It is advisable to add an overflow pipe at the lower end. Run the pipe through a hole next to the drain, and make the top of it flush with the top of the growing medium. Either tie it into the drain pipe, or run it directly back to the sump. Place a 1 by 2 block under one end of the box to tilt the box toward the drain.

Since the growing bed is generally placed on a bench in the greenhouse, the other apparatus—a small plastic garbage can or bucket to hold the nutrient solution and a small electric pump—can go under the bench. The pump is submersible and sits at the bottom of the solution container.

Connect the pump to a timer that is set to flood the box once in the morning and once in the evening. The box will fill to the top, and it should drain in 10 or 15 minutes.

It is a good idea to sterilize the bed at least once a year. Mix 1½ ounces of liquid chlorine in 10 gallons of water. Plug the end drain hole and fill the box until the growing aggregate is fully submerged. Let it soak 24 hours, then drain and throw away the chlorine solution. Flood and drain the box with fresh water three times a day for the next two days. Then you're ready to plant again.

PROJECTS FOR CHILDREN

These special projects—from planting a terrarium to growing a pineapple—are intended to be both fun and educational. Schedule them for inclement weather when children can't go out to play.

Terrarium

Planting and caring for a terrarium—a glass-encased garden that is, in effect, a miniature greenhouse—gives children an appreciation of nature and teaches them something about the way plants grow.

Almost any plant can be planted in a terrarium as long as it is small enough to fit inside. Fishbowls, brandy snifters, candy jars, and aquariums are among the many types of containers that can be used for a terrarium.

Planting the terrarium begins with sprinkling some woodsy soil or potting mix in the bottom of the container. A few bits of charcoal should be added to keep the mix from getting musty. Then, armed with plastic bags, take the children on a plant hunt to the woods, a meadow, a swamp, or someone's backyard. Whatever the location, make sure you have permission to gather plants there and that you aren't removing any endangered species.

Encourage the youngsters to observe how the plants are growing so they can try to create a natural scene in the terrarium. Let them collect tiny clumps of moss, evergreen seedlings, ground covers such as vinca or wintergreen, and even weeds such as veronica or chickweed. The plants should be lifted carefully so the roots are intact.

The children can gather colorful stones, odd pieces of wood, lichen, and bark (from the ground, not from a live tree). Small mirrors can serve as lakes and streams when tucked under moss or grass. Small amounts of perlite or white sand can be used for special effects.

After the terrarium has been planted, it should be watered carefully so that the soil is moist but not muddy. Cover the terrarium. If too much moisture builds up, adjust the cover to leave a small opening. Lack of condensation means that water should be added. If watered properly, the terrarium won't need moisture again for a few weeks.

Place the terrarium in bright light, but not hot sun. It should be turned regularly so that all the plants receive enough light.

These young girls are learning how to take care of plants. The greenhouse will provide them with hours of fun and education during rainy or cold weather.

Other Fun Projects

The greenhouse can be a great learning experience for children. Some simple projects consist of recycling fruit remnants into living plants. Other projects include creative ways to grow different kinds of seeds.

The learning experience will be more valuable if the children care for and nurture the projects they've planted. Teach them how to water, fertilize, and groom their plantings.

Avocado   An avocado pit can be grown into a fine foliage plant. Choose a variety that is dark skinned and pear shaped; it will form roots quickly. Wash the pit and let it dry for two or three days. Jab three toothpicks equally spaced, midway between the top and bottom, and suspend it in a glass of lukewarm water so that the bottom is always wet. As an alternative, you can bury the pit in a loose potting mix; the pointed end should be up and the dimpled end down.

Coffee tree   Few plants are showier than a coffee tree in bloom or bearing fruit. The plant has fragrant white flowers followed by colorful reddish or purplish berries. Sow unroasted

Left: This pineapple plant must be kept evenly moist if it is to produce fruit.
Right: The seeds in the pixie pie plate have sprouted, creating a jungle landscape for toy figures.

seeds, purchased from a seed supplier or organic food store, in a mixture of sand and peat moss. Transplant each seedling into a 4-inch pot, and move it into larger pots later as necessary. In the greenhouse, a coffee tree will grow 4 or 5 feet tall.

Olive   Select pits from black olives; these are sure to be ripe. Speed up germination by nicking the bony seed coat with a file and freezing the pits in ice cubes for three weeks. Then plant the pits in a pot containing a mixture of sand and peat moss.

Date palm   The date palm has a bony seed, which can be found in packaged dried dates. Wash the seed and carefully file a small notch (until you see white meat) in the seed coat. Then bury it about 1 inch deep in a loose potting soil. If you don't nick the seed coat, it may take a year for germination. Since the date is a desert plant, give it the warmest spot in the greenhouse and keep the soil just barely moist.

Pineapple   Select a fresh pineapple that has green tufts, not straw-colored ones. Twist off the top, or slice it off with about ½ inch of flesh attached. Remove any fruity part, being careful not to injure the tough stem in the center. Let the top sit in a shady spot in the kitchen for about a week. Then press it into potting mix in a 5-inch pot.

Place the potted pineapple in a part of the greenhouse where the temperature is at least 60° F (16° C) at night. Keep it moist; a misting

every few days is helpful. It can be shifted to a larger pot in about two months, just after roots have formed. Fertilize about once a month.

Fruit forms in about 20 months. When the plant is about 18 inches tall, you can coax it to bloom and form fruit by placing an apple on top of the pot. Ethylene gas given off by the apple triggers the flowering. Enclose the plant and apple in a plastic tent and move it to a shady spot so that heat does not build up inside the plastic. After one week, remove the plastic and notice new growth—the edible fruit—starting to form in the center of the plant.

Pixie pie plate   Cut a piece of flannel or terry cloth to fit the bottom of a large pie plate. Draw pie slices with a soft pencil, and sprinkle different seeds on each pie slice. Use seeds from the kitchen cabinet—celery, caraway, and mustard, etc.—or any tiny leftover flower seeds.

Each pie slice will sprout in its own time; there will be a pattern of different colors and textures. Keep the cloth very damp at all times, and give the seedlings a spot in the greenhouse where they will get bright light.

Garden in a glass   Line the inside of a water glass with blotting paper. Add just enough water so that the blotter is damp enough to cling to the sides of the glass. On the blotting paper place a variety of small seeds or larger, flat seeds such as cucumber; you can also use seeds from a birdseed mix. Keep water in the bottom of the glass. The seeds will soon sprout and fill the glass with plants.

U.S. Measure and Metric Measure Conversion Chart

	Symbol	Formulas for Exact Measures When you know:	Multiply by:	To find:	Rounded Measures for Quick Reference		
Mass	oz	ounces	28.35	grams	1 oz		= 30 g
(Weight)	lb	pounds	0.45	kilograms	4 oz		= 115 g
	g	grams	0.035	ounces	8 oz		= 225 g
	kg	kilograms	2.2	pounds	16 oz	= 1 lb	= 450 g
					32 oz	= 2 lb	= 900 g
					36 oz	= 2¼ lb	= 1000 g (1 kg)
Volume	pt	pints	0.47	liters	1 c	= 8 oz	= 250 ml
	qt	quarts	0.95	liters	2 c (1 pt)	= 16 oz	= 500 ml
	gal	gallons	3.785	liters	4 c (1 qt)	= 32 oz	= 1 liter
	ml	milliliters	0.034	fluid ounces	4 qt (1 gal)	= 128 oz	= 3¾ liter
Length	in.	inches	2.54	centimeters	⅜ in.		= 1 cm
	ft	feet	30.48	centimeters	1 in.		= 2.5 cm
	yd	yards	0.9144	meters	2 in.		= 5 cm
	mi	miles	1.609	kilometers	2½ in.		= 6.5 cm
	km	kilometers	0.621	miles	12 in. (1 ft)		= 30 cm
	m	meters	1.094	yards	1 yd		= 90 cm
	cm	centimeters	0.39	inches	100 ft		= 30 m
					1 mi		= 1.6 km
Temperature	°F	Fahrenheit	% (after subtracting 32)	Celsius	32° F		= 0° C
	°C	Celsius	% (then add 32)	Fahrenheit	212° F		= 100° C
Area	in.²	square inches	6.452	square centimeters	1 in.²		= 6.5 cm²
	ft²	square feet	929.0	square centimeters	1 ft²		= 930 cm²
	yd²	square yards	8361.0	square centimeters	1 yd²		= 8360 cm²
	a.	acres	0.4047	hectares	1 a.		= 4050 m²